General editor: Graham Handley MA Ph.D.

Brodie's Notes on George Orwell's

Animal Farm

I. L. Baker BA

MACMILLAN

First published by James Brodie Ltd
This revised edition first published 1990
by Pan Books Ltd

Reprinted 1992 by
THE MACMILLAN PRESS LTD
Houndmills, Basingstoke, Hampshire RG21 2XS
and London
Companies and representatives
throughout the world

ISBN 0-333-58159-8

Printed in Great Britain by
Clays Ltd, St Ives plc, Bungay, Suffolk

Page references in these Notes are to the Penguin
edition of *Animal Farm*, but references
are also given to particular chapters, so that
the Notes may be used with any edition of the novel.

Contents

Preface

The intention throughout this study aid is to stimulate and guide, to encourage your involvement in the book, and to develop informed responses and a sure understanding of the main details.

Brodie's Notes provide a clear outline of the play or novel's plot, followed by act, scene, or chapter summaries and/or commentaries. These are designed to emphasize the most important literary and factual details. Poems, stories or non-fiction texts combine brief summary with critical commentary on individual aspects or common features of the genre being examined. Textual notes define what is difficult or obscure and emphasize literary qualities. Revision questions are set at appropriate points to test your ability to appreciate the prescribed book and to write accurately and relevantly about it.

In addition, each of these Notes includes a critical appreciation of the author's art. This covers such major elements as characterization, style, structure, setting and themes. Poems are examined technically – rhyme, rhythm, for instance. In fact, any important aspect of the prescribed work will be evaluated. The aim is to send you back to the text you are studying.

Each study aid concludes with a series of general questions which require a detailed knowledge of the book: some of these questions may invite comparison with other books, some will be suitable for coursework exercises, and some could be adapted to work you are doing on another book or books. Each study aid has been adapted to meet the needs of the current examination requirements. They provide a basic, individual and imaginative response to the work being studied, and it is hoped that they will stimulate you to acquire disciplined reading habits and critical fluency.

Graham Handley 1990

The author and his work

George Orwell was the pseudonym adopted by Eric Arthur Blair in his late twenties (for reasons later to be mentioned): but it will be convenient throughout this compressed biography in particular, and in all the later notes generally, to refer to him by his more familiar name of Orwell.

Orwell was born (25 June 1903) at Motihari in north-west Bengal, the only son of Richard Walmesley Blair, a minor official in the Opium Department of the Indian Civil Service, and Ida Mabel Limouzin. Both parents were of Scots extraction, and their two other children were daughters, one older and one younger than the boy. His mother returned to England with the children when Orwell was quite young, and he hardly saw anything of his father until he was eight, when Blair returned to England on retirement: Orwell remembered him as 'a gruff-voiced elderly man, for ever saying "Don't"'.

The young boy – like the older Orwell – was lonely, driven in upon himself, unable through shyness to reveal his innermost feelings, even to his mother. At the age of eight he was sent to a preparatory school on the south coast, where he remained until he was twelve. Orwell was unhappy there for various reasons about which one can only speculate, although no doubt his introspection, sensitivity, 'middle-class' background and the beginnings of a lung complaint must have been contributory factors. Nevertheless, he won two scholarships, and chose the better one to Eton, where he stayed during the years 1917–21. Orwell said of these years, 'I did not work there and learned very little, and I don't feel that Eton has been much of a formative influence in my life.' However, we do know that he was a popular pupil there, making many friends (some of whom later became celebrated writers and critics, and who were to be useful contacts). Orwell was good at games and joined fully in the school's social life: later on in life he praised Eton's tolerant and civilized atmosphere and its fine traditions.

It would have been normal for Orwell to have gone up to Oxford or Cambridge after Eton, but, acting apparently on a master's advice, he left to enlist with the Indian Imperial Police in Burma. Orwell spent five years there, and later embodied his experiences and sensitive reactions in his first novel, *Burmese Days*. Several other pieces of writing, notably the two essays, 'Shooting an Elephant' and 'A Hanging', also draw heavily on his Burmese experience. In general he ridiculed and indicted much of the process of British rule in Burma, feeling that Imperialism – indeed, any and all power exerted over people – was an evil to be resisted. He spoke of 'evil despotism' and an 'oppressive system', and felt guilt in his authority. Orwell left Burma on leave, never to return, in 1927, and for several years after seemed to be working off his guilty conscience and shedding his past by plunging into a series of menial jobs and a tramp-like existence in London and Paris. In his *Down and Out in Paris and London* the reader glimpses his extreme poverty, and his knock-about life as a dishwasher, a private tutor and a teacher in cheap private schools; as a tramp, mixing with the squalid and the sordid in dosshouses and workhouses.

It was about this time that he changed his name for his literary work (though never by deed-poll) from Eric Blair to George Orwell. This, too, was possibly a further deliberate action to break himself away utterly from his past, to attempt to live almost as a new personality. Some writers have attempted to adduce further reasons, commenting on his pseudonym as a typically English name (think of the patron saint of England and the Suffolk river named Orwell near to the writer's own home), in contrast to the Scottish ring of his baptismal name. There is also some evidence that Orwell disliked the Scots and their country, while he revealed a great and genuine love for England. It is profitless to pursue the topic further, for the individualistic Orwell rarely dwelt on such personal topics, even to his closest friends.

The following years brought a number of books, such as the novels *A Clergyman's Daughter* (1935) and *Keep the Aspidistra Flying* (1936), which impressed the critics but did not sell well. Fond of such detail, Orwell calculated that between the years 1930–40 his literary earnings did not quite amount to three pounds a week, despite considerable contributions to many magazines and journals. In 1936 Orwell moved into possession of a village 'pub' and store in Essex (he always hated London), and on the strength of slightly increased earnings, although he reckoned that he rarely made more than one pound a week profit, he married. He abandoned his store when the publisher Victor Gollancz commissioned him to go to the north of England to write a documentary on the condition of the unemployed. The resulting book, *The Road to Wigan Pier* (1937), was a disconnected, rather contradictory and, to Gollancz's embarrassment, often bitterly anti-Socialist study of social problems in a depressed area. The book was fiercely honest, Cobbett-like in its denunciations, and often sincerely yet utterly wrong in its historical lack of balance: and it provoked considerable interest and criticism.

However, even before the book's publication Orwell had left for Spain, where the Civil War had broken out in 1936. In December he had set off for Barcelona, ostensibly to serve as a journalist for the publishing firm of Secker & Warburg. In fact, he joined the militia in a small group, a curious non-Communist Socialist brigade known as the POUM (*Partida Obrero de Unificación Marxista*), one of the three existing units then engaged. Orwell's *Homage to Catalonia* (published 1938) is both autobiography and history. He was wounded while in the front line: a sniper's bullet passed through his neck and narrowly missed his windpipe by about a millimetre. The wound left Orwell's voice 'cracked' for the rest of his life. More significant, however, was the way in which the war opened Orwell's eyes to the means and ends of the Communists, their intrigue and treachery, their lies, libels, expedient denunciations and falsifications. These Orwell never forgot, and such experiences coloured and strengthened and in a way reoriented and reorganized his future political beliefs, emphasizing in particular his belief in the essential decency of man, were it allowed to triumph over political and social intrigue and cant.

Orwell returned from Spain in the summer of 1937, and for the following two years lived quietly in Hertfordshire (apart from a trip to Morocco in the winter of 1938), writing and gardening. He had always suffered from consumption, and his war-wound no doubt aggravated his ill-health, from which he was now never to be free.

His next novel (published in 1939) was *Coming Up for Air*, and featured a fictional biography of a cheerful boozy middle-aged insurance salesman who tries, with little success, to relive the happiness of his boyhood. The novel is interesting and significant in the author's development, as it stresses those political and social elements which, in Orwell's view, had caused the uneasy armed peace between the two Great Wars, and which had made the Second World War inevitable and imminent. The book met with some success, running into several editions which came, indeed, into the period of the beginning of the Second World War, which Orwell had prophesied in 1934.

Orwell's next publication was a long essay on Charles Dickens (now included in *Critical Essays*), an important, stimulating, often provoking piece of critical assessment, essential reading for any student of Dickens (and of Orwell, too, for that matter). Orwell persistently volunteered for military service but was always rejected on grounds of ill-health: he nevertheless joined the Home Guard, and became a sergeant. In 1941 he joined the Indian service of the BBC, broadcasting often from underground, artificially lit and airless studios. Despite his poor physical condition, there is reason to believe that both he and his wife went regularly without their rations so that others should have more. A bitter consequence of this was the collapse, after a quite minor operation, and death of Orwell's wife during the last year of the war.

After this personal tragedy, and for the last months of the war, Orwell travelled abroad as a correspondent for *The Observer*. During the period between November 1943 and February 1944, he had written *Animal Farm*, which was published in the very month of the German surrender in 1945. The satire caught the public fancy, running into many editions and translations, and providing Orwell for the first time in his life with a reasonable income. As much of the rest of these Notes considers this work in detail there is no need to comment here on its nature and impact.

Many other essays and works followed, notably those on *James Burnham and the Managerial Revolution* (1946) and *The English People* (1947), a long and interesting essay with some pertinent comments on the English language. He also contributed a regular weekly article to the *Tribune* magazine under the title of 'As I Please' between December 1943 and February 1945, covering a wide range of political, social and literary topics. Orwell's last work (although some collections were collected and published posthumously) was *1984*, a particularly grim novel. This pessimism can be attributed to both Orwell's ill-health and tiredness aggravated by a stay on Jura, a remote island off the west coast of Scotland, in the worst possible conditions for a consumptive. *1984*, a popular book later to be televised and filmed with considerable impact, is the terrifying story of a possible future, with England (merely 'Airstrip One') a grim totalitarian governed state in a world intermittently at war. Everything and everybody is supervised and controlled: 'Big Brother' is forever watching; a Ministry of Truth re-writes history as is convenient and expedient; human love is eradicated; power is the object of policy as an end in itself; there is constant irresistible propaganda and even an authorized version ('Newspeak') of the English language.

During the last months of his life Orwell remarried, and made plans for new work, particularly a book on Joseph Conrad. He intended to fly to Switzerland to recuperate from his lung trouble. A day or two before he was to leave, on 23 January 1950, he had a haemorrhage and died within a few minutes.

In a number of ways Orwell, the writer and the man, stands out as an interesting, curious and rather isolated figure. An Etonian, he was also a socialist, but a theoretical socialist who (unlike another, G. B. Shaw) never sacrificed truth on the altar of humour or effect, and one who vigorously denounced the shortcomings and the egalitarianism of academic socialism. Again, he saw himself largely as a political pamphleteer: 'Every line of serious work I have written since 1936 has been written, directly or indirectly, *against* totalitarianism and *for* democratic socialism, as I understand it.' Few such writers have ever been as fearlessly honest, or as versatile, or as constantly preoccupied with the purity of their prose, as was Orwell. Of good family and background, though not rich (as we have seen), and of a shy, reserved and introspective nature, Orwell deliberately plunged into a life with social outcasts. Despite his own highly individualistic belief in socialism, he considered that no honest writer could attach himself to any political party. A patriot, at times even a fervent and sentimental patriot, Orwell endlessly criticized (among other things) the English inability to think logically, the English class-consciousness and the English lack of artistic ability.

Further, Orwell was an idealist, though more of a 'breaker of idols' than one who contrived practical substitutes: but with his idealism there ran a realism, a matter of factness, a staring of facts in the face which usually resulted in pessimism. He hated materialism, and yet his views on spiritual impulses, and on organized religion generally, were highly sceptical. For these and indeed other equally and apparently paradoxical reasons Orwell would seem to present an insuperable problem to anyone attempting to distill some basic belief, some fundamental radical philosophy. It is equally difficult to attach some literary label to the whole range of his works, which included some six novels, two largely autobiographical, lengthy critical and political pamphlets, forty main essays on many topics and countless contributions of the more ephemeral kind to many magazines.

Yet there is, again perhaps paradoxically, no great problem here, for one trait does shine through, growing and developing from first to last. This is what may be called a sense of decency (Orwell's favourite word): a feeling for honesty and truth, and linked with it, a search for freedom, especially political, social and intellectual freedom separated from cant, humbug, bigotry , hypocrisy and expediency. It is as he himself said of Dickens: 'His whole message is one that at first glance looks like an enormous platitude: If man would behave decently the world would be decent.' And from another essay: 'Either power politics must yield to common decency, or the world must go spiralling down into a nightmare, of which we can already catch some dim glimpses' (this was written in 1943).

The performance and recognition of decency and honesty and loyalty towards one's fellow-man is the key: not expediency, unfulfilled intention or escape into abstraction. The fact that the world, for many, is harsh and brutal is because such fundamental decency and loyalty have been deliberately, usually politically, banished or exploited by seekers after power. Orwell never deluded himself: hence his discomfort at the political and social tendencies of the totalitarian and mass advertising age, based largely on exploitation and power tactics. His burning love of truth, as he saw it, made him an uncomfortable goad to the indifferent, complacent or malevolent. *Animal Farm* was written and published at a time when the West was an ally of Russia (herself an ex-ally of Hitler's Germany), when Stalin was still a popular figure as 'Uncle Joe', and when real disillusionment with Russia was just beginning. Thus its writing and timing in themselves seem typically Orwellian gestures.

George Orwell requested that no biography of him be written:

none of his many friends, devotees and literary critics betrayed that trust. Instead they published reminiscent and authoritative studies which included fragmentary items of biographical detail culled from his own works. However, in 1980, Bernard Crick published *Orwell: A Life*, a full-length, scholarly biography covering all the significant detail of Orwell's life and writings. Despite this mass of analytical and critical interpretation, for most readers a problem seems to remain. It is still difficult (for in his own work Orwell does not always explore his own motives) to understand Orwell the man. Much of his work is bitter, reflecting disappointment and disillusion, and by *Nineteen Eighty-Four* has a touch of hysterical despair. From this one might guess that Orwell himself lived out his life equally sourly. It is necessary to correct this impression.

To his friends the adult Orwell was sociable and home-loving, believing in family life: though he had no children of his own, he adopted a son, and was concerned greatly for his education and future. Orwell was selfless, naturally mild and gentle; though his chronic consumption, war-wound and deliberate self-denial over rations led to some physical emaciation in his later years, it can be said that he enjoyed life to the full whenever he was physically and financially able to do so. He read as widely as he could afford: he smoked and drank. One of his friends, indeed, once referred to him as a 'Public House' rather than a 'Public School' character, being tall, lean and scraggy and 'the least Etonian character who has ever come from Eton'.

Many commented on Orwell's awkward boyishness, his fundamentally shy and retiring personality. Apart from writing, he enjoyed tinkering, although he did not like machinery. Above all, he confessed that gardening, especially vegetable gardening, was his favourite occupation outside his work. He was sensitive, physically and mentally, with an acutely observing eye and, it must be noted, an acute nose. He was particularly sensitive to smell: in his works he never omits to indicate, sharply and expressively, the smell pervading the places; he himself was not squeamish in adult life.

Orwell loved animals, and it has been suggested that this affection toned down much of what could have been sharper and more bitter in *Animal Farm*. Other friends commented on his dry humour and his curious 'rusty' laugh. Exaggeratedly perhaps, but significantly, one of his friends called him a 'saint'.

Orwell once wrote, 'A man only stays human by preserving large patches of simplicity in his life', and we see the blend of the man and his work in his unbounding sympathy for the troubles of all political, social and religious victims of snobbery, oppression and persecution. His fierce honesty and passionate pursuit of truth angered many, but made countless friendships among all sorts and conditions of men: and even his enemies grew to respect him.

Radical and swift movements in the post-war world (in politics, economics, social welfare) have continued to inspire a remarkable revival of interest in Orwell's writings and attitudes. What amounts to a 'cult' of Orwell has arisen; many books, talks, articles have been produced on aspects of Orwell's life and works. The reason is clear. The ominous persistence of power politics, the 'cold war' tensions and battles in the Middle East inflamed by opposing idealogies, the imposition of the Kremlin's will upon its post-war 'satellites' (until very recently), local but bloody wars and frontier clashes in the Near and Far East – all these have underlined Orwell's clear and prophetic insight into the nature of naked aggressive power, and the cynicism of its wielders. Greatly advanced systems of communication such as television and satellite relays – even from the moon's surface – which can influence the minds of millions; the intensification of nuclear and germ war research, the struggles of various post-war socialist governments in Europe to establish more egalitarian but non-Communist states: so much of this is already implied in the works of Orwell (especially in *Animal Farm* and *1984*) that critical reassessment of his works is timely and proper. This has been given a strong impetus by the publication of his collected works in a definitive edition, and especially by the four volume gathering of all Orwell's occasional writings, essays, journalism and letters by his second wife Sonia Orwell, assisted by Ian Angus (Secker & Warburg, 1968).

Plot

The animals of Mr Jones's Manor Farm, incited partly by neglect but mainly by the revolutionary dreams and anti-human doctrine of the prize boar old Major, strike when the opportunity arrives and free themselves from all their human taskmasters. The pigs assume leadership, under Napoleon, Snowball and Squealer. The animals are directed and organized, and a constitution is set up. Everyone sets to work to effect a Utopia, especially the cart-horse Boxer, and the farm continues successfully enough, with regular meetings, committees and classes. The dominant pigs already seem to be doing less of their share of the real labour, yet grasp and retain more of the increasingly rare privileges.

Later on in the year, Mr Jones and some local men attempt to take the farm by force: they are beaten off in what comes to be called 'The Battle of the Cowshed', in which Snowball is wounded. Some animals desert the farm, but the outstanding issue is the fight for leadership mastery between the two rivals, Napoleon and Snowball, who advocate contrary policies. Napoleon, however, gains sudden command by a practical demonstration of brute force: at his call some dogs he has been training from birth for this purpose, attack Snowball and chase him permanently from the farm. Napoleon is now in complete mastery, with Squealer as his servile mouthpiece and apologist.

Napoleon decides to build a windmill, which supposedly will ease everyone's labours: but its building is a slow and laborious process, despite Boxer's herculean and tireless efforts. Contact is also to be made through a Mr Whymper (a local solicitor) with the outside world of humans for the purposes of trade. The pigs eventually move into the farmhouse, previously out of bounds: they sleep in its beds, and one of the early Commandments is found to have been consequently and suitably amended. One stormy night the windmill collapses, and Napoleon claims that Snowball is responsible, and in his absence sentences him to death. Another windmill is to be built forthwith.

A hard winter follows, and rations are reduced, although the outside world is deliberately misled about such conditions. The sinister renegade Snowball is held responsible for any short-comings or crises, and it is even said that his secret agents lurk in Animal Farm. One day, indeed, Napoleon and his dogs execute all those animals who have shown any reluctance or resistance to the new regime, and only Boxer's great strength and immediate retaliation saves him from death. Another of the Seven Commandments is found to have been altered.

Napoleon, now self-styled 'The Leader', enjoys a lofty eminence and isolation. He negotiates the sale of some timber to neighbouring farmers, endlessly playing off one against the other. Eventually the sale is made, for cash, but in forged notes. This offensive transaction heralds a further attack by the humans on Animal Farm. In 'The Battle of the Windmill' the humans are chased off, but the windmill is blown up and many animals are killed.

The pigs, the ruling class, acquire a taste for alcohol after an unpleasant initiation, and yet another Commandment is altered.

Boxer, staunch supporter of the initial principles of the regime, works beyond his strength, looking forward to his imminent retirement. One day he collapses, and his final reward is to be taken off to the knacker's yard, though Squealer details smooth words and facile lies about his last hours in hospital.

The Animal Farm republic grows old: few pre-Revolutionaries remain alive, and the farm thrives through the hard toil and depressed conditions of the labouring animals, who still dream of old Major's Utopia, a Republic of equal animals. But a decisive change occurs when the pigs begin walking on two legs in direct imitation of man, and take to carrying whips. Even that bond of equality has been broken, and the pigs readily acquire more and more human attributes and accessories. One day some local farmers, after a tour of inspection of Animal Farm, are entertained by the ruling pigs. The workers look in on the happy self-congratulatory scene. Humans and pigs are playing cards and drinking, and some speeches are made, extolling the pigs' discipline of and mastery over their own 'lower classes'. Napoleon's terse and relevant speech announces various changes in the established order, including a reversion to the old name of 'Manor Farm'. Cheering and applause are followed by argument and quarrelling, ostensibly over cheating at cards: and the watching animals find to their horror that they are unable to distinguish between the features of the humans and the pigs.

Historical and political background

Historical background

Orwell finished *Animal Farm* in February 1944, but the book was not in fact published until May 1945, the month and year of the end of the war with Germany. This delay was because it had been successively rejected by four publishers; however, the timing of its eventual publication by Secker and Warburg enhanced its success, and it quickly ran into many editions and translations. In order to understand this aspect of its popularity and, further, to see the book as a satire, even an anatomy and dissection of the Soviet system, one must look a little more closely at two historical sequences: the contemporary background of the war years 1939–45, and the general pattern of Russian history in its Revolutionary period 1917–27 and its Stalinist period 1924–53. One point must, however, be made clear. It is difficult to write of the USSR's post-Revolutionary history without appearing wrong-headed about or even malicious to one ideology or another, so widely separate have the systems of belief become since 1917. The best corrective is a reading of material from both 'sides'. Here we shall try to concentrate on what seem to be the 'facts' in their plainest interpretation, and refer to the text of *Animal Farm* whenever and wherever parallels suggest themselves. The various personalities (and some institutions) concerned will later be considered in greater detail.

The Second World War (1939–45) started, so far as the fighting was concerned, with Germany's invasion of Poland on 1 September 1939. That lit the spark, but the combustible materials had long been laid with the League of Nations' failure to check military invasions and conquests of several Powers, such as the Japanese invasion of Manchuria in 1931; the Italian attack on Abyssinia; the German, Italian and Russian intervention in the Spanish Civil War; Japan's undeclared war on China; Germany's invasions of the neutralized Rhine, of Austria, the Sudeten lands, Czechoslovakia and Memel; and Italy's conquest of Albania. Hilter and his 'Axis' colleague, Mussolini, dictators of

Germany and Italy respectively, were redrawing the map of Europe almost at will. The invasion of Poland, however, before an impossible ultimatum had expired, provoked Great Britain and France to action, and within one day the Commonwealth also declared war on Germany in support of Poland. That country was extinguished within three weeks: Russia, under a secret clause of the Russo-German pact of August 1939, advanced from her 1921 frontier to occupy eastern Poland and Germany occupied the rest.

The haggling and intrigues of Germany's Hitler and Russia's Stalin (compare the Napoleon-Pilkington-Frederick episodes of the book) were bearing fruit. Russia next demanded bases from Estonia, Latvia, Lithuania and Finland: the first three submitted, and were admitted as soviet republics of the USSR: Finland refused, the Russians campaigned (not entirely successfully) and secured a few more miles of land. The uneasy 'phoney' war now followed, with a quarter of a million British troops across the Channel poised on the Belgian frontier. Better weather heralded a massive German offensive, and between 9 April and 1 June 1940, Hilter's armies invaded Denmark and Norway, the Netherlands, Belgium and Luxembourg, defeated France – pushing the British force into the Dunkirk evacuation – occupied the Channel Islands, captured Yugoslavia and occupied Athens and Crete, apart from North African enterprises with Italy, and Japanese invasions in the Far East. Then, at dawn on 22 June 1941, Germany attacked her ally Russia without warning. The unholy alliance between Nazism and Communism fell apart at one crushing blow.

There is no room here to trace the ebb and flow of the epic struggle between these colossal forces, the Germans pushing up to the very gates of Leningrad in the north and Stalingrad in the south. A total Russian effort, with all her civilians at war, the peasants burning their homes and crops so that the enemy should not enjoy their use, and the sacrifice and suffering of all her people, who were given short shrift even as official prisoners-of-war: all this was a fantastic and amazing effort, which was backed up (although this has never been fully acknowledged by the Russian leaders or detailed to the Russian people) by great material assistance from the Western allies, culminating in the Allied invasion of Europe in June 1944.

The tremendous struggle of the Russians under their leader

Stalin (see p.24) impressed everyone, often to the point of envy. Her enormous sacrifice and sufferings were obvious, her absorption and containment of massive German forces decisive, and, in her eventual counter-attacks, her retribution on her ex-allies, the Germans, was considerable. All this induced among her allies, and the masses of people generally, an unbounded admiration for 'Uncle Joe' Stalin, a reticent, pipe-smoking, homely-looking man, and his peoples. But Orwell, who had seen Russian activity in Spain, was less impressed and Russian intransigence over a multitude of problems soon changed the old wartime collaboration into mutual suspicion and irritation, resulting in tensions and fears in the 'cold war' that followed. Orwell, of course, did not live long enough to see the full disillusionment and ominous development of this suspicion and hostility: but his previous experiences, his acumen, his acute political flair, and his faith in that elusive 'common decency' which could bring men together in harmony, made him a prophet. He had already written such telling lines as:

All talk about democracy, liberty, equality, fraternity, all revolutionary movements, all visions of utopia, or "the classless society," or "the Kingdom of Heaven," are humbug (not necessarily conscious humbug) covering the ambitions of some new class which is elbowing its way into power.'

'In each great revolutionary struggle the masses are led on by vague dreams of human brotherhood, and then, when the new ruling class is well established in power, they are thrust back into servitude.'

'History consists of a series of swindles, in which the masses are first lured into revolt by the promise of Utopia, and then, when they have done their job, enslaved over again by new masters.'

Animal Farm, as a political satire, is an essay on this theme. It is also a light-hearted portent of what was to be Orwell's final work, *1984*, in which bitterness and desperation reach a climax, typified by such lines as, 'Power is not a means, it is an end. One does not establish a dictatorship in order to safeguard a revolution: one makes the revolution in order to safeguard a dictatorship. The object of persecution is persecution. The object of torture is torture. The object of power is power.' And, terribly, 'If you want a picture of the future, imagine a boot stamping on a human face – for ever.'

Finally, as *Animal Farm* at one level is a thinly-disguised political satire on the Russian Revolution and the later Stalinist period of Russian history, one must comment briefly on these topics. The reigning Tsar (and the last Tsar of Russia) at the beginning of the First World War was Nicholas II (1868–1918). Like his predecessors, he believed in his divine right to force a stern, repressive, bureaucratic autocracy on the 120 million people of Russia (compare Mr Jones), and disaffection was rife, culminating eventually in the summoning of a national assembly to discuss constitutional reform. Nothing useful happened, as the Tsar would not weaken his authority through three successive assemblies of wrangling – the fourth was in session when the war began. The army was ill-equipped; the constitution faltered and tottered; and disorders swept away tsardom with all its hangers-on.

With the collapse of the monarchy, various political movements assumed greater significance, the most important being Communism, under Lenin (see p.25). Under him, in the October Revolution, the Bolsheviks (the radical and majority Communists) seized power. Slogans abounded: the state seized all the means of production; the land and the banks were nationalized.

Lenin and his second-in-command, Trotsky (see p.26), had established 'the dictatorship of the proletariat'; or, rather, a small group of political manipulators were bent on putting into action the code of Marxism (see p.26). The Cheka, later to be called the OGPU (see p.23), was organized to suppress counter-revolution. (Compare and re-read *Animal Farm*, Chapters 1–4.) In addition the Church was disestablished and a strong 'Godless' movement created, and all ranks and titles were suspended. Lenin then concluded a separate peace with Germany at Brest-Litovsk (March 1918), losing territory and contributing further to economic crisis. A period of civil war followed between the 'reds' and the 'whites' – opposing leaders, with the 'whites' supported by many foreign troops, including British, French, Polish, and American, attempting to suppress Bolshevism (compare the neighbouring farmers of *Animal Farm*). In the long run they were defeated by the red army, organized and led by Trotsky (compare 'The Battle of the Cowshed', Chapter 4). The Tsar, Nicholas II, and all his family were assassinated.

Russia was economically exhausted, and Lenin's hopes that the spark kindled in Russia would lead to world Communism showed no hope of being realized. He then abandoned militant Communism, and introduced the new economic policy (NEP) which restored some measure of private enterprise; the Treaty of Rapallo, signed with Germany in 1922, broke the boycott of Soviet Russia by the capitalist world (compare Napoleon's dealings with Willingdon markets and Whymper, Chapter 6). Lenin died in 1924, and a struggle then followed between his personal lieutenants Stalin (see p.24) and Trotsky, based on personal, political and tactical rivalry. Stalin eventually drove all his opponents from power, and in 1927 Trotsky himself and his associates were expelled from the party, and then banished (compare the end of Chapter 5). Through various 'purges', often accompanied by 'confessions', Stalin exterminated all those of the Lenin circle during the years 1936–8 (compare text, especially end of Chapter 7). The first five-year plan (the 'windmill' theme of *Animal Farm*) was introduced in 1928, its purpose being to develop new industries, collectivize agriculture, and develop Russia as a modern industrial state. After much opposition, especially from the peasants, the plan got under way, to be followed by others in series up to the beginning of the Second World War. Of Stalin's career more detail will be found in the section under 'Napoleon', p.24.

It will thus be readily seen that *Animal Farm*, re-read with this background in mind, is an attack on the Russian Revolution and Stalinism; and it is the Socialist Orwell attacking from the Left, basing his attack on reality and historical fact, a great deal of which has been exposed in recent years by Russian leaders themselves in their 'De-Stalinization' programme. Events have indeed confirmed Orwell's exposures in greater measure and accuracy than one would have wished. In his own controlled way, Orwell tells us 'how it happened'; and a great deal of his political thinking and feeling is contained in the text's few pages.

Political background

This is not the place to digress at length on political philosophy and ideology, either historically and in general, or in particular from *Animal Farm* or any other of Orwell's works in which such topics are involved. One or two relevant points may be noted. The whole business of the State and the individual, of who is to govern whom, how and why, with what checks and balances, has

been a crucial topic throughout the centuries, argued theoreti-
cally and philosophically from the time of the Greek city-state,
Herodotus and Plato, to modern 'isms'; and often argued, too,
physically and violently, by war. Fundamentally it is a question
of power: in whom it is vested, how it is wielded, who has to
submit or succumb in some measure, and who is to succeed.
Some of Orwell's views on power have already been quoted.

Animal Farm, as a political satire, is a controlled and unexag-
gerated account of power politics, aimed in particular at the
Russian experiment and in general at any 'revolution' which
springs from Utopian promises (and which do not?). It is important to note, however, that Orwell considers the 'Revolution' to
have *failed*. The regular compromises made by the pigs to the
fundamental principles of Animalism, and the equally (and consequent) retrogression of the farm animals into a new servitude,
prove that it has failed. They have merely exchanged one whip-
handed tyrant for another: and it is in fact rather worse, for the
new masters are of their own kind, and not external exploiters.
The fact that the whole regime is different in pattern does not
necessarily make it better. Animalism, Communism, Fascism –
what you will – so far as the mass of people is concerned, turns
out to be a hollow progress, a barren achievement, a Pyrrhic
victory, despite the 'bread and circuses'. A new hierarchy
replaces the old, and the new is but the old writ large.

Note, too, that Orwell never for one moment suggests that the
old regime is a good one, or that the revolutionaries were not
justified in kicking over the traces. Jones and his men are
drunken and lazy, and no doubt more brutal than they need be:
the mere threat of their return is enough to quell the restless
and disturbed. For a true freedom and a real independence the
animals (except Mollie) are prepared to sacrifice much: and they
in fact sacrifice freedom itself without understanding how and
why it has been filched from them: only their goal remains as a
vision, a Utopian dream, just as it was at the beginning for old
Major. The wheel has turned full circle, and the whole movement has been in the nature of a colossal deception.

One final point. The scholar and historian, Lord Acton
(1834–1902), once wrote, 'Power tends to corrupt: absolute
power corrupts absolutely'; this was his considered opinion after
many years of historical research and reading. The generaliz-
ation has the ring of truth, especially to modern ears, and the

progress of, say, Naopleon and Squealer in *Animal Farm* seems to comment wryly on the essential truth of the maxim. It may, however, be argued (and it is still being argued) in actual historical contexts whether this is all the truth: whether or not Hitler or Stalin or Mussolini, to consider recent times alone, did rise in power not merely of and through themselves, but because their peoples wanted them so to rise. Popular support and backing encouraged and fortified them in their endeavours for supreme overlordship.

Animal Farm, too, considers this theme in its own way, and finds it wanting. There must be leaders, certainly, policy-makers and tacticians: and the mass of people must believe and support. But the point clearly demonstrated by Orwell is that these leaders pervert and distort the truth, lose touch with the people at large, and dupe them for base motives. Masses of people can be wielded and moulded by propaganda, once the intelligent and rebellious have been purged, and power thrives on the human perplexity and bewilderment consequent on such propaganda striking home. Good-natured and gentle as the satire often is, this exposure of deliberate corruption is all too familiar and none the less bitter.

The following alphabetically arranged list brings together some of the major political and other allusions and references of the text: it should not be assumed, however, that the text implies or attempts to imply all these details, or even follows them with accuracy historically. They are merely suggestions which Orwell possibly had in mind while writing his satire, and textual parallels will readily come to mind through several close readings of the text itself.

'Beasts of England'

This recalls the international anthem of the Communist parties, and, until 19 December 1943, the national anthem of the USSR. It is usually called *L'Internationale*: the original words were written in French in 1871 by Eugene Pottier, and it was set to music about twenty years later by Pierre Degeyter, a Lille artisan. The first verse of the English version reads:

Arise, ye starvelings, from your slumbers;
Arise, ye prisoners of want!
For reason in revolt now thunders

And at last ends the age of cant.
Now away with all your superstitions;
Servile masses, arise, arise!
We'll change forthwith the old conditions
And spurn the dust to win the prize.

Refrain
Then comrades, come rally
And the last fight let us face:
The Internationale
Unites the human race

About 1946 the anthem was replaced by one stressing the idea of Russian patriotism, although it was retained as the party anthem.

Old Major's song may well also be a playful Orwellian parody (of sorts) of a poem by P. B. Shelley (1792–1822) who, in an age of European republican and revolutionary activity often wrote material of what we might call 'protest' or 'anti-Establishment' flavour. The poem is called 'To the Men of England': one stanza reads:

The seed ye sow, another reaps;
The wealth ye find, another keeps;
The robes ye weave, another wears;
The arms ye forge, another bears.

Boxer
The 'willing horse' is an excellent example of what used to be called in Russia a Stakhanovite, now almost an unknown term in the USSR. Alexei Stakhanov was a Russian miner who regularly exceeded his quota, his 'norm' of output, and he was held up to other Russian workers as an example. Stakhanovites were given higher wages, certain rewards, and some special privileges: but penalties were imposed for the under-fulfilment of norms. There was great abuse of the system, for propaganda purposes, by the establishment of very low norms which were bound to be exceeded, and sometimes they were lowered so as to disguise a reduction in wages. The system was exposed as 'fictitious' after Stalin's death (1953) but was revived in part by the formation of 'Teams of Communist Labour'. The USSR has long been more concerned with all-round production rather than individual feats of record-breaking.

The Dogs

These represent the Cheka (Chrezvychainaya Kimissiya), a police department first organized by Lenin, the 'Extraordinary Commission for Combating Counter-Revolution, Sabotage and Speculation'. This force, later to be developed into the dreaded OGPU, engaged in punitive terror and formidable mass liquidation of State 'enemies', and was involved, often as police, prosecutor, judge, jury and executioner – all in one – in many of the great purges.

Jones

In general, Jones represents Tsardom, mentioned elsewhere (see p.18). Nicholas II (1868–1918) was the last Tsar of Russia: he was, in fact, a kindly man, quite unfitted for his high office. Convinced of the divine right of kings, he allowed some constitutional reforms in an attempt to quell dissatisfaction with the government's policy, but he nullified them by subsequent actions. The First Great War exposed the internal weakness of the regime, and he unprotestingly signed his abdication in 1917. He was arrested and interned, with his wife and five children, transferred to the Urals, and all were assassinated in July 1918. The corpses were removed to an isolated spot and burnt.

Minimus

Many USSR writers were prompt to 'toe the party line', and use their art in elevation and praise of its basic revolutionary and industrial principles. Under Stalin's dictatorship, creative work dried up. The Ode to Napoleon (Chapter 8) has its parallel in, say, a *Hymn to J. V. Stalin*, which includes the lines,

The world has no person
Dearer, closer.
With him, happiness is happier,
And the sun brighter.

Moses

In many ways Moses sums up the fluctuating attitude of the USSR to religious practice. The Soviet system remains officially atheist, but permits surviving churches, of many persuasions, to pay their own way through their collections: they also pay taxes. No religious instruction is permitted for persons under 18, and none in schools or institutions. Nevertheless there are some

20,000 churches and 18 religious seminaries open (1986 figures), and the Communist authorities have in practice adopted varying policies at different times towards different religions, with gradual concessions. Apart possibly from that which affects the Jews, no active or even subtle persecution, on religious grounds alone, is evidently promoted by the government. In recent years, indeed, many restrictions have been entirely relaxed.

Napoleon

Napoleon represents Stalin (1879–1953). Josef Vissarionovich Dzhugashvili, born in Georgia, of peasant stock, was a member of the Bolshevists from the beginning (1903) and adopted the alias Stalin (Man of Steel). He combated Tsarism, and was repeatedly imprisoned and eventually exiled to Siberia. After the Revolution he became a member of the Political Bureau of the Communist Party under Lenin, becoming in 1922 General Secretary of the Central Party Committee. After Lenin's death in 1924, Stalin and Trotsky struggled for succession: Trotsky believed in world revolution, Stalin in *Russian* socialism. Trotsky was expelled from leadership of the Soviet Union in 1929: relentlessly pursued by fanatics, he was later assassinated (see 'Snowball', p. 26). Then followed Stalin's series of Five-Year Plans: industrialization was applied on a massive scale, and, on the agricultural side, some twenty-five million individual peasant holdings were concentrated or 'collectivized' into communal and state farms, against colossal resistance which was ruthlessly crushed: some ten million peasants, at least, were deliberately starved or executed for non-conformity. In 1934 began the purges, the elimination of all possible enemies and malcontents, with millions pressed into forced labour: a Party purge in 1936 and 1937 resulted in the executions of former leading Communists.

Stalin himself was deified, and permitted a cult of his own personality to foster and develop, especially as he represented the champion of anti-Nazism, describing Germany as an aggressive nation as late as 10 March 1939. Nevertheless, on 23 August 1939, while actually negotiating an alliance with Britain and France, Stalin concluded a non-aggressive pact with Hitler, the dictator of Germany, giving the German Führer a free hand in Poland, and later joining in that country's partition. Then he secured virtual control of Estonia, Lithuania and Latvia, and invaded Finland (see p.16). Russia's participation in the Second Great War has already been mentioned. This gruff man of great will and ruthless achievement made the Revolution a success, on his terms. It has been said that Stalin was probably responsible for more deaths than any other man in history, except possibly Hitler and Genghis Khan, and, from what was said by Krushchev at the Twentieth Party Congress in February 1956, there is little reason to doubt the suggestion.

Old Major

Major represents a mixture of Lenin and Marx. Vladimir Ilych Ulyanov (1870–1924) organized and led the October Revolution, and was the founder of both the Communist Party and the Soviet Union: he translated the Marxian philosophy into practice and action, cutting through millions of Marx's words to fundamental propositions, such as the creation of the party; the overthrow of bourgeois supremacy; the setting up of 'the dictatorship of the proletariat'; the introduction of socialism; and the basic conquest of political power. He assumed the name Lenin in his early revolutionary days. His father was a high-ranking inspector of schools and his mother a doctor's daughter, and his early environment was well-to-do and intellectual. He became a lawyer and a strict Marxist: Lenin lived in exile as a Bolshevik, and was returned to Russia by the Germans, becoming the leader of the Bolshevik Party. With Trotsky, he organized the first unsuccessful uprising, but the 'October' Revolution succeeded in overthrowing the existing government, and the Council of the People's Commissars took its place, with Lenin as its President. Civil war ensued until 1921, the Bolsheviks, now called Communists, winning the day; and Lenin, under his New Economic Policy (NEP) admitted some private initiative and profit, and even private enterprise. This was liquidated in 1927 in favour of a strictly socialistic Five-Year Plan policy.

Lenin was shot at in 1922: his health deteriorated, and, mainly in consequence of overwork, he fell ill and died. His body was embalmed, and is on permanent exhibition at the Lenin Mausoleum in Moscow, on the western side of Red Square. Some of his maxims are: 'Promises are like pie-crusts – made to be broken'; 'It is necessary . . . to resort to all sorts of stratagems, manoeuvres, illegal methods, to evasion and subterfuge, only so as to get into trade unions, to remain in them and to carry on Communist work within them at all costs'; 'Give me four years to teach the children, and the seed I have sown will never be uprooted'; 'It is true that liberty is precious – so precious that it must be rationed.'

There is something of Marx, too, in Orwell's presentation of old Major. Heinrich Karl Marx (1818–83) was a German economist and the founder of international revolutionary socialism. In 1847 he drew up the manifesto which may be regarded as the foundation of modern socialism, and his classic work on socialist economics, *Das Kapital*, in three volumes, dealt basically with the theory of surplus value: Marx claimed that a workman's labour possesses more intrinsic value than is required to support him, and that the surplus is filched from him by exploiting capitalists, which is their profit. Thus there is nothing in common between the employers and the employed, the proletariat: the latter must therefore develop a class-consciousness and unite, eventually to wage a class war in which the whole capitalist system would be overthrown. Marxism considers economic conditions as the basis of life: political and other systems merely being a 'super-structure' which undergo changes along with them. One quotation is worth reproducing: 'The workers have nothing to lose in this (Revolution) but their chains. They have a world to gain. Workers of the world, unite!'

The Pigs

These, as the government, parallel the Commissars, 'The People's Commissariat of Internal Affairs', their Russian name usually abbreviated to the NKVD. Their history is complicated, but, in the early days, they were a development of the Cheka (see 'The Dogs', p.23), and were responsible for internal administration, including the charge of some police work, troops and militiamen, and registration activities. They also commanded labour power.

Snowball

Snowball represents Trotsky (1877–1940), the alias of the Russian Bolshevist leader, Lev Davidovich Bronstein. Banished to Siberia, he escaped in the third year of his exile to join Lenin: once more arrested and banished, he escaped again, living in various European countries until he rejoined Lenin in the successful Revolution of 1917. With Lenin Trotsky seized the reins of government and established the Council of the People's Commissars (see above), with Lenin as president and himself as Commissar for Foreign Affairs. From 1918 until 1925 he was Commissar for War, but his influence declined after Lenin's death in 1924, and Stalin gradually ousted him from all his posts. In 1927 Trotsky was expelled from the Party and in 1929 he was expelled from the country. He lived for a while in France and later settled in Mexico, where he was assassinated in 1940. Constantly criticizing Stalin's policies, denouncing Stalin as a traitor to Communism, and even writing a book called *The Betrayed Revolution*, in which he hoped a new uprising would end Stalinism and restore true Communism, it seemed inevitable that he would not be tolerated under Stalin's ruthless system.

Windmill
The whole business of the windmill recalls the economic plans of Soviet Russia, usually called the Five-Year Plans. The first (1927–32) provided for the creation of basic industries, while later ones concentrated on processing industries and consumer goods.

Animal Farm and satire

Typical of the many judgements passed on *Animal Farm* are the following: 'Good-natured satire upon dictatorship'; 'Bitter and destructive as this fable is ...'; '... this curious parable'; ',,, its symbolism obvious but not blatant'. Each of these is worth some consideration, but, before pinning any literary 'label' on the book, it may be of use and interest to consider some aspects of fable and humour in general and satire in particular. The mere literary tag is not enough.

In the first place, *Animal Farm* is a *fable* simply in the sense that it is a story with a message and meaning in which animals act as if they were humans. Examples of modern writing in which animal characters reflect human affairs are works such as H. G. Wells's *Island of Dr Moreau* and Capek's *Insect Play*. It must be noted here, and noted very carefully indeed, that in *Animal Farm* the nature of the animals' 'beastlike' characteristics is emphasized: the eventual progress by the pigs, however inevitable, to the two-legged human stance is a sudden climax, amazing and terrifying to the rest of the normally quadrupéd farmworkers. This point will be mentioned again.

Secondly, the book is an *allegory*: the animals' condition and situation represent not just a human state, but a particular class of humanity, a particular society (Revolutionary and post-Revolutionary Russia) in a specific situation. Again, the animals may be taken to represent all or any people of any place and time, and the inevitability of events under certain conditions and circumstances. Clearly this shows that the book is along the traditional lines i.e. composed in 'receding planes'. This means that is has an appeal and a meaning at various levels. Swift's *Gulliver's Travels* is a stock example of this. At one level, it is a humorous, at times exciting and astonishing yarn which quite small children can enjoy. At the next level, it can be read as a bitter attack on many social, moral and constitutional abuses, as any annotated edition will demonstrate; while at another level, it can be interpreted as a withering attack on 'man's ingratitude to man' with invective and biting sarcasm flaying human complacency and stupidity. So is it with *Animal Farm* (which has, however, more in common with the voyage to the Houyhnhnms than with the rest of Gulliver's journeys). It is perhaps less notable as a children's book, though it can be regarded – as indeed the author called it – a 'fairy tale': perhaps the message and intention obtrude too sharply, and it lacks some of the diversity and yarn-like adventurous quality of Swift's work.

Finally, however, the book is a telling *satire* on the Stalinist period of Russian history. It is a warning and a portent of what seems to Orwell the inevitable fate of mankind, given certain conditions, and the ultimate objective of power-seekers and demagogues of any country. It is the climax of the overthrow and exploitation of common decency: as such it is a prelude to the desperation of *Nineteen Eighty-Four*. *Animal Farm* has been called 'a work of genius in the lofty tradition of English humorous writing'. This comment serves as a useful springboard for further dissection of the nature of the book.

If we define humour as having discovery for its motive, its scope being human nature, its method observation and its audience the sympathetic, *Animal Farm* is clearly humorous. It reveals the way in which demagogues seek to obtain power and explores the humbugging and hypocritical methods used to meet this end; yet we, the audience – the 'willing horses' of our own political and social systems – can sympathize with the inevitable failure to achieve Utopia. Much of the book is wryly comic, for example the portentous Major with his pseudo-political meeting (Chapter 1), Snowball's Animal Committees (Chapter 3), the pigeon's opening attack on the humans (Chapter 4) and the creation of decorations (Chapters 4 and 8).

There is some wit, particularly in the amendments to the original Seven Commandments of Animalism, where the addition of an odd word alters, in the most obvious and comprehensive manner, the original concept (Chapters 6, 8, and again in 10) culminating, splendidly and how inevitably, in the climax of 'All Animals are equal – but some are more equal than others'. There is little room for further wit, for this reveals itself particularly in sophisticated conversation and word-play, not a feature of this animal-cum-human fable. Orwell is too objective and restrained, and perhaps he loved animals too much, to indulge here in irony and sarcasm, except of the most controlled and modified kind. Faults and foibles are, of course, exposed, but these are held up rather to gentle chiding and ridicule than flayed without mercy: but this very understatement, this negative aspect (remember or look up the terms 'litotes' and 'meiosis') serves to heighten and emphasize what he is positively asserting and intending. The same good-humoured control prevents invective. A good deal of the pigs' misconduct is, of course, discredited, but not always directly and often by implication.

The general method of the entire book, however, is the deliberate exaggeration – to the point of ridicule and absurdity – of the new society's ethics and behaviour, suggesting all the time a comparison with what we understand generally to be the more humane, the better, the more correct and civilized, the more acceptable codes of human morals and manners. This is the principle of satire. The literary history of satire dates from the Romans: it is the only literary form which they may be said to have invented. Through the ages, from Juvenal and Lucilius; through Erasmus' *In Praise of Folly* and reaching the heights in Voltaire's *Candide*, Rabelais' *Gargantua* and *Pantagruel*, Cervantes' *Don Quixote* and Swift's *Gulliver's Travels*, writers have attempted to improve society, or at least expose it, by mocking its follies and vices with fierce indignation and savage mockery.

The late seventeenth and entire eighteenth centuries were the great ages of English satire, though mainly in verse. Samuel Butler's *Hudibras* inveighed against hypocrisy; Dryden's *Absolom and Achitophel* flayed Lord Shaftsbury and his party; and Pope, in various works, ridiculed everything, polite society and tasteless extravagance in particular. The form was continued by such as Dr Johnson in his *Vanity of Human Wishes*, and Byron's general rebellion against cant and hypocrisy: and Butler's *Erewhon* is a satire on all the political and social Utopias hankered after by man through the ages. In our own country, whenever the form of satire is considered, three names will always be to the fore: Evelyn Waugh (e.g. his *The Loved One*); Aldous Huxley (e.g. his *Apes and Essence*, and another glimpse into the future, *Brave New World*); and Orwell, sprung from Swift but differing in his motivation and conviction.

A close reading of the following passages of *Animal Farm*, and, if need be, their linking with what information is provided elsewhere concerning the political background, will indicate the essentially satiric nature of the whole story.

Chapter 1   'At this moment . . . voted on both sides.' (p.6)
Chapter 2   'The work . . . of the animals.' (p.9)
Chapter 3   'The attempt to tame . . . kept their distance.' (p.20)
Chapter 5   'He was especially . . . save the labour of cartage.' (pp.31–2)
             'That evening . . . without further questions.' (pp.38–9)
Chapter 6   'All that year . . . reduced by half.' (p.40)
             'Curiously enough . . . proper perspective.' (p.45)
             'With one accord . . . upon Snowball.' (pp.47–8)
Chapter 7   The whole episode of carnage and confession.
Chapter 8   'On Sunday mornings . . . two other anniversaries.' (pp.61–2)
             'Meanwhile the timber . . . for nothing!' (pp.67–8)
             'As they approached . . . booming of a gun.' (p.70)
             'About this time . . . would say nothing.' (p.73)
Chapter 9   'Meanwhile life was hard . . . part of the time.' (pp.74–7)
             'Three days later it was announced . . . case of whisky.' (pp.83–4)
Chapter 10   'The farm was more prosperous now . . . were always good.' (pp.86–7)
             'It was a pig walking on his hind legs . . . wear on Sundays.' (pp.89–90)
             'It was a source of great satisfaction . . . to say which was which.' (pp.91–5)

A careful reading and re-reading of these extracts will indicate the varieties and potentialities of satiric writing.

Structure and style

Structure

Very little needs to be said in detail on the structure of *Animal Farm*, as this is strongly linked with its style. Two factors need, however, to be noted: the time-sequence of the plot and what may be called the 'narrative timing'.

The time-sequence offers a good example of Orwell's belief in the principles of clear prose: no doubt is left in the reader's mind as to where or when events are occurring. Place, of course, is limited to the bounds of the farm. Throughout the book, more importantly, one can see how the time-sequence is made clear. From these references it can be shown that all the events take place within a three year span up to the beginning of the final chapter, when Orwell writes 'Years passed'. Details are carefully provided of the months and seasons, with special reference to the farming year; and the whole story unfolds evenly and chronologically. The student might well gather the references in sequence, such as 'early in March', 'next three months', 'all through that summer', and so on.

Of perhaps greater interest is what may be called Orwell's 'narrative timing'. A great deal of the plot of *Animal Farm* would appear shaky and faulty if logical conclusions and sequences were fully pursued. For example, it is obvious more invading humans would eventually overpower the animals; self-sufficient farming consists of more than milking, sowing and harvesting; the windmill construction, both in theory and practice, would soon have halted over technical problems insuperable even to the most intelligent of animals. But Orwell skilfully avoids getting involved in such detail and with problems for they would hold up the intention and pace of the story. Re-read, for example, the episode of breaking down the stones for the windmill (Chapter 6), and note how the process is taken only so far: what is unsaid, about further complications of collection, haulage, sorting, lifting and so on, is deliberately unsaid.

Linked with this is the timing and the picking-up of threads and ideas before they have had a chance to be forgotten. The result is a subtle criss-crossing of material, brought out for emphasis or climax as the occasion demands. This is done with great skill, and one or two examples may suggest lines of enquiry. Note, for example, the detail of old Major's speech (Chapter 1), and then consider how, throughout the book, various aspects of it are re-echoed, usually satirically. It is almost as if it had been written last (though there is, of course, no evidence of this) as a deliberate parody of all that follows. Again, note the moment of the reintroduction of the dogs; the occasions on which 'Beasts of England' is sung; the whole windmill sequence; the recurrent details of Foxwood and Pinch-field and their owners; the details of which the 'purge' is a climax; the retrospective allusions to pre-Rebellion days and ways; the use of the sheep in the chorus. These and similar elements are introduced in a logical and meaningful pattern. In this way the basic ideas of the book are never allowed to flag or become forgotten. This 'timing', this skilful bringing into notice or emphasis relevant material at the accurate and opportune moment, is a feature easily overlooked, a first-rate instance of 'art concealing art'.

Adaptations from one literary medium into another generally involve radical changes in structure: it may thus be worth mentioning that *Animal Farm* has been adapted for both radio and film. It was first broadcast in the then quite new Third Programme of the BBC in January 1947: Orwell himself made the radio version, using the device of an impersonal narrator to link the story. Later versions (by the original producer, Rayner Heppenstall) revised Orwell's arrangement, and made Clover the storyteller. The cartoon film of *Animal Farm* aroused great interest. Maurice Denham 'supplied' all the animals' voices, and once again, a narrator was used. The film was on 'unfixed release' in 1955 which meant, in effect, that it was not put into general circulation, its run depending entirely on public interest and support. However, the film entirely altered the ending of the original novel by giving the story a happy ending, in which the animals of the world unite against Napoleon in a second revolution, and expel him. It will be clear from a reading of these Notes that this represents a complete reversal of Orwell's thesis.

Style

Any professional writer such as Orwell must be interested in language and matters of style: but Orwell is exceptional in that he is not merely interested in, but sincerely concerned with and for, the English language. A great deal of his writing, directly and indirectly, is taken up with illuminating and often provoking remarks on this topic. Orwell confessed that *Animal Farm* was 'The only one of my books I really sweated over', and, further, that it 'was the first book in which I tried, with full consciousness of what I was doing, to fuse political and artistic purpose into one whole'. It thus deserves particular attention to its linguistic and stylish aspects.

To begin with, however, it might be useful and interesting to gather together some of Orwell's comments on the English language.

So long as I remain alive and well, I shall continue to feel strongly about prose style.

Good prose is like a window-pane.

To write or even to speak English is not a science, but an art.

Whoever writes English is involved in a struggle that never lets up even for a sentence. He is struggling against vagueness, against obscurity, against the lure of the decorative adjective, against the encroachment of Latin and Greek, and, above all, against the worn-out phrases and dead metaphors with which the language is cluttered up.

It must also be remembered that Orwell is in the literary tradition of the political pamphleteers, and that a great deal of his thinking was political and sociological. He felt that language had a vital part to play in clarifying thought and opinion. Hence, 'one ought to recognize that the present political chaos is connected with the decay of language, and that one can probably bring about some improvement by starting at the verbal end'; and, 'If you simplify your English, you are freed from the worst faults of orthodoxy.'

Orwell was intensely interested in words, especially in their manipulation in propaganda, and in *1984* he indicated how the official language Newspeak could become a major instrument of tyranny. He did eventually formulate a few rules which he thought writers should observe. They are:

1 Never use a metaphor, simile or other figure of speech which you are used to seeing in print.

2 Never use a long word where a short one will do.
3 If it is possible to cut a word out, always cut it out.
4 Never use the passive where you can use the active.
5 Never use a foreign phrase, a scientific word or jargon word if you can think of any everyday English equivalent.
6 Break any of these rules sooner than say anything downright barbarous.

Observant readers will notice the similarity (and extension) to the precepts recommended by H. W. and F. G. Fowler in their standard work *The King's English.*

1 Prefer the familiar word to the far-fetched.
2 Prefer the concrete word to the abstract.
3 Prefer the single word to the circumlocution.
4 Prefer the short word to the long.
5 Prefer the Saxon word to the Romance.

Orwell's fundamental interest, however, went beyond all this. He campaigned throughout his life for clearer thinking and clearer writing. His belief in 'common decency' was allied to the utterance and expression of the unvarnished truth, and Orwell turned his theories of language into practice by aiming at a style and diction, largely achieved in *Animal Farm*, in which it would be impossible to tell lies, a style so hammered and strong that any humbug and insincerity would at once be obvious and obtrusive. This conscious intention makes Orwell's prose flexible, clear, forceful and forthright.

Minor blemishes can indeed be found, but not easily. Orwell's otherwise ample and sharp vocabulary fails a little, perhaps, in his over-use of 'said': some thirty-three out of sixty-four 'verbs of saying' in the entire book are, rather colourlessly and lamely, just 'said'. There is equal loss of force (in a language particularly rich in shades and tones and nuances in its 'verbs of saying') in the uses of 'cried', 'exclaimed' and 'asked'. There is a strong repetition, too, of the word 'three' in the plot's sequence: 'Three nights later', 'three months', 'three days later' (used three times, in fact), 'on the third Sunday'; this could have been varied a little more. One or two sentences read a little awkwardly, such as, 'He took them up into a loft, which could only be reached by a ladder from the harness-room', where 'only' is misplaced; 'Now if there was one thing that the animals were completely certain of . . .' is a little clumsy with the preposition slung at the end; 'They were the same pigs as had protested' is a little uncomfortable in its conjunction; 'there were days when they felt that they would sooner have had less figures and more food', in which 'fewer' could better replace 'less'. There is also as tendency to begin many sentences with 'And' and 'But', and very many with the interjection 'Yes', devices perhaps commoner (and better) in speech than in writing.

However, when all this is said, and it is not much, it is well to remember that we are dealing (as Buchan said of Sir Walter Scott) with a master, and not a schoolmaster, of language. The virtues of Orwell's style preponderate enormously above such minor faults. Apart from the defects mentioned, the vocabulary is sharp and apt, and indicates a close observation and apprehension of the exact word. Taking the first page of the text as an example, note the sharp accuracy of such terms as 'popholes', 'dancing', 'lurched', 'ensconced'. Note, too, the scarcity of descriptive adjectives and qualifying adverbs: but where such extensions are employed, they are strong (e.g. within Chapter 1: 'benevolent', 'vast hairy hoofs', 'stout motherly mare', 'cheeping feebly', 'mincing daintily' etc.).

We have already considered the sequence, logical, and chronological, of the plot: the notions of where, when, how much, how many, how long in any reference or situation are always clear. There is no ambiguity: no important detail omitted; there is no sudden abandonment of any theme. The paragraphing, and the sentence construction within the paragraphs, is varied and never monotonous: the links too are logical and intelligible. The punctuation is clear for sense and sound: re-read old Major's speech (Chapter 1), observing the punctuation in detail, and see how it contributes to the rhythm and pulse of the whole.

Orwell is sparing in his use of figurative language, but what examples do appear are appropriate, sharp and not distracting (e.g. 'the ring of light from his lantern dancing from side to side'). One of the graces of Orwell's prose is that it is particularly literal (apart, of course, from the underlying satire), and what might be called level, in that it does not burst out into any 'purple passage' or rhetorical flight. Three extracts deserve special attention in this light, where it would have been easy for Orwell to have overspilled into elaboration and sentiment. They are the animals' panoramic view and consideration of Animal Farm which might be taken as an Orwellian view of his beloved England, which is seen in contrasting moods: 'But they woke at dawn ... all their own' (p.13–14); 'The animals huddled about Clover ... words to express them' (p.58–9); 'And yet the animals ... All animals were equal' (p.87–8). The virtues of literalness, control and tightness of language are here expertly and wonderfully demonstrated: language does not have to be high-flown, ornate or allusive to be moving.

The bare bones of the story are cleverly concealed by circumstantial detail, which helps to translate the fable-like structure and message into real and human terms. We thus see and appreciate the characters as the animals they are, though they represent humans in human situations. Orwell draws in realistic, often detailed, background scenes, so that we can suspend (or even forget) our disbelief in the literal impossibilities of the basic idea. Particularly strong and telling examples of this are to be found in the setting of old Major's speech (Chapter 1), the scenes of the farm and farmhouse (Chapter 2), the details of the harvest (Chapter 3), the whole campaign of the Battle of the Cowshed (Chapter 4), and, of course, the long-drawn-out sequence concerning the windmill and its fate (Chapters 5, 6, 7 and 8)). A great deal of this detail supports and reinforces the satire, and those satirical passages already listed should be explored for this blend of background information and satire. This provision of relevant circumstantial detail also forms part of Orwell's conception and basic principles of clear prose, in that no doubt is left in the reader's mind as to the exact situation of circumstances. It is all explicit, specific and immediately acceptable; unambiguous, clear and sharp. It often reveals what one critic called Orwell's 'dilatory eye': there is a momentary pause, a minor delay in the movement and sequence of events, so that relevant material may be adequately supplied on some significant topic.

The pace of the narrative deserves comment. It should be noted how, in straightforward description, the detail accumulates swiftly, pushed on at speed towards a sharp climax, often terminating in some telling sentence. In this respect the opening and close of each chapter are noteworthy; but internally too, the device keeps the story going, covering a great deal of ground in a little space, brought up every now and then to a sharp peak. Some examples (there are others) are: old Major's speech (Chapter 1) terminating in the exciting singing, and then the drunken shot of Mr Jones; the 'Revolution' itself (Chapter 2); Snowball's expulsion (Chapter 5); the exposure of Squealer (Chapter 8); the Boxer episode, especially Chapter 9, 'However Benjamin and Clover . . . empty'; and the final scene (Chapter 10).

Note, too, that Orwell's style (and here *Animal Farm* is generally representative) is capable of varying use: it can describe and argue, criticize and explain.

Summarizing, then, the main characteristics of Orwell's style here are its simplicity and directness; it has pace and zest, but is never loose, uneven or out of control. His style is pithy and purposeful, accomplishing its satire nimbly and without hysteria, and its symbolism is never obvious or blatant. It is above all clear and unaffected, an honest style; strong, economical, diverse and versatile. Unlike the prose style of many justly celebrated authors it is a first-rate model for the aspiring writer to try to imitate. But this does not deflect from the uniqueness of the story: its systematic satire serves a serious political purpose; it is as technically perfect as any creative writing can be. In its style, diction and structure *Animal Farm* reveals what has been called Orwell's 'love affair' with the English language. A 'fairy tale' at one level, and a stark satire at another, it throughout exposes and expresses the lonely, fierce courage and honesty of its author.

It is perhaps too soon to attempt to 'set' Orwell in his place in English literature; he has shown himself to be a gifted political pamphleteer and satirist, critical reviewer and novelist, sociological and war reporter, autobiographer and essayist. It is easier to look back rather than forward, and try to trace some of the influences which may have affected him in his thinking and style.

We know from his own works which writers he cared for most: Shakespeare, Swift, Fielding, Dickens, Charles Reade, Samuel Butler, Zola, Flaubert, and the moderns James Joyce, T. S. Eliot and D. H. Lawrence. He considered that the one writer who influenced him most was Somerset Maugham, in his power of telling a story straightforwardly and without frills. The legacy of some of these is easy to trace, even in the short space of *Animal Farm*, which we have seen to be strong and economical. Clearly the satire of *Animal Farm* was influenced directly by Swift, especially his *Tale of a Tub* and *Gulliver's Travels* (particularly the voyage to the Houyhnhnms).

There is something of Cobbett, too, in Orwell's radicalism and love of the common man, and in his violent denunciation of abuse and insincerity: and Cobbett was another serious student of the English language. There is also something of the keen but level temper and love of democracy of Hazlitt; and the pace of much of his work is reminiscent of Sterne, who may perhaps be said to have first introduced vigour and thrust into English prose. The literary student will find hints of Shaw and H. G. Wells in Orwell's humour, politics and general approach: and something of the serious and sombre 'grey' style of Gissing also seems to have affected some of his writing.

Apart from the obvious legacy of Swift, there is one other English writer to whom surely Orwell owed much. *Animal Farm*, in its light-heartedness and smoothness, in its delightful creation of scenes of animal life, vivid, realistic and set in really absurd situations; betraying a warm and sincere love of the animal world, yet direct, wry, observant and sharply serious: all this is strongly reminiscent of Chaucer. One feels that these two Englishmen, separated by six centuries, would have understood each other perfectly.

Chapter summaries, textual notes and revision questions

Chapter 1

One night in early March old Major, the prize boar of Mr Jones's Manor Farm, summons a meeting of all the animals in the big barn. Eventually they all muster, including the cart-horses Boxer and Clover, Muriel the goat, Benjamin the donkey and Mollie the white trap-mare. Major tells them that before his death, which he feels to be imminent, he must impart some of his wisdom, and furthermore tell them of a dream he has had.

Old Major then explains in some detail how the nature of their lives, and the lives of their children, is unnecessarily servile and laborious, wretched and short. Man, their supreme parasite and enemy, is the sole cause. With unity and comradeship they could prevail over him utterly, and establish an animal kingdom in which all animals are equal. His dream is of the Utopia consequent upon Man's banishment and defeat. Major sings a traditional song, 'Beasts of England', which epitomizes the blissful future for which they will have to struggle. The animals are wildly excited, quickly grasping and repeating the song in their various voices.

The tumult arouses the drunken Mr Jones, who thinking that a fox might be in the yard, fires off a reckless shot from his bedroom. The animals scuttle to their several sleeping places and go to sleep.

pop-holes Small cut-out doorways.
Middle White A breed of pig, compact, with a short head and turned-up snout, chiefly in demand for the pork trade.
Willingdon Beauty A typical 'show' name for farm animals. There is a Willingdon in Sussex.
tushes Long pointed teeth.
eighteen hands Horses are measured in hands, a unit of four inches. This height is measured to the shoulder.
our lives ... short Compare this with a sentence from Thomas Hobbe's *Leviathan* (1651), an exposition of political philosophy: 'And the life of man, solitary, poore, nasty, brutish, and short' (Chapter 13).
porkers Young hogs fattened for the pork market.
knacker One who buys and slaughters old and useless beasts. Horses

are often bought and 'boiled down' for animal (especially cat's) food.
'Clementine' Popular ballad by Percy Montrose.
'La Cucuracha' Popular song of the thirties from a film of the same name: written by Juan Y D'Lorah in 1934, it is a lively rumba.

Chapter 2

Old Major dies three nights after the meeting, and three months of feverish activity follow, organized by the more intelligent animals, especially the pigs: the Rebellion must be prepared for. Two young boars, Napoleon and Snowball, with a persuasive porker named Squealer, formulate old Major's precepts into a philosophy called Animalism. Despite some stupidity and opposition, the belief prevails. The Rebellion itself happens quite spontaneously as a result of Mr Jones's neglect: he, his wife and all the farmhands abandon Manor Farm to the united, infuriated and truculent beasts, who then can hardly believe their wonderful success. All traces of human oppression are destroyed.

The next day they rejoice further in their freedom: the farmhouse is inspected, and they decide never to use it for animal habitation. Snowball and Napoleon, who have educated themselves, rename the farm 'Animal Farm', and write out the Seven Commandments, the basic principles of the new order. Already, however, there are signs that the pigs are taking advantage of the gullibility of the other animals.

Berkshire A breed of pig, named after the English county. The breed is black but for the face, feet and tip of the tail: it is a hardy pig, profitable to keep, producing fine hams.
linseed cake i.e. the cake which remains when the oil is pressed out of flax seed, used as a food for sheep and cattle.
Windsor chair A type of strong plain polished chair, made entirely of wood.
News of the World A Sunday newspaper, founded in 1843, specializing in extensive coverage of crime and other sensational events.
carpet bag Travelling bag made of carpeting.
castrate To remove the testicles.
spinney Small wood or thicket.
Brussels carpet Type of carpet of wool pile and with a stout linen back.
lithograph A picture printed by a method called lithography, a process of obtaining prints from stone or metal surfaces treated in such a way

that what is to be printed can be inked while the remaining area rejects ink.

Queen Victoria Queen of Great Britain and Ireland for sixty-three years (1819–1901), Queen Victoria succeeded to the throne just after her eighteenth birthday. Her long reign and widowhood, personality and prestige, endeared her to her people.

Revision questions on Chapters 1–2

1 What is the gist of Major's speech?

2 How are Napoleon and Snowball already differentiated in character and temperament?

3 What is the function of Squealer and Moses in these chapters?

4 What indications do we already have of Napoleon's opportunism?

Chapter 3

After enormous effort, organization and improvisation a bumper hay harvest is gathered: the summer passes happily enough. Boxer, in particular, despite his limited intelligence, proves his devotion to the cause by long and strenuous physical efforts. On the Sunday holiday the green flag, with its hoof and horn symbol, is hoisted, and the Meeting takes place, in which the pigs, led by Snowball and Napoleon (who disagree fundamentally with each other), plan out the next week's work.

Animal Committees are set up for organization and 're-education', and a degree of general literacy is achieved. A new comprehensive slogan is adopted ('Four legs good, two legs bad'), learned off and endlessly repeated by the sheep in particular. Napoleon concentrates on the young, and personally takes charge of a new litter of dogs. The pigs have the best of the milk and fruit, on the grounds that they, the brain workers, need always to be in perfect condition for their burdensome responsibilities. Their failure, it is repeatedly emphasized, would herald the return of Jones, a fate too dreadful to contemplate.

Chapter 4

News of the events at Animal Farm spreads: neighbouring farmers, especially Mr Pilkington of Foxwood and Mr Frederick of Pinchfield, each on bad terms with the other, fear the rebellion and spread false rumours about it. The Revolutionary tendencies, and the rousing, hopeful song, are widely known among other farm animals. Early in October news arrives by pigeon that Mr Jones, armed with a gun, is leading a party of men, obviously intent on recapturing his farm. However, the animals have prepared a pre-meditated pattern of skirmishes and pretended retreat. The final charge is led by Snowball who is shot at and wounded, a sheep is also killed, and Boxer, unwittingly and with regret, fells a stable-lad (who is, in fact, not killed but stunned, for he later hobbles away). They have won the day: the flag is hoisted, 'Beasts of England' sung, the dead sheep given a hero's burial, and Boxer and Snowball are decorated for their gallant defence in what is henceforth to go down in history as the Battle of the Cowshed.

had their females in common i.e. shared wives. While this was never true generally, the early Russian Revolutionaries held the marriage relationship in complete contempt, and divorce was granted automatically at the mere request of either party. Much more stringent laws apply today.

Julius Caesar Roman soldier and statesman (102–44 BC); a most skilful soldier and strategist.

muted Discharged their excrement.

Chapter 5

Winter approaches. Mollie, the vain trap-horse who has always hankered after her sugar and ribbons (luxuries and marks of class and mankind long condemned), deserts Animal Farm, and is never mentioned again. The next season's work is planned by the pigs, but, Snowball and Napoleon cannot agree on essentials, and allegiance is divided.

The building of a windmill on the highest point of the farm is one such bone of contention. Snowball sees it as a centre of power leading directly to greater leisure: Napoleon believes that food production should be their paramount concern. They disagree further over the future defence of the farm, Napoleon wishing to obtain firearms and Snowball believing in stirring up outside rebellion. The windmill project is debated at a mass meeting: Snowball's eloquence is just winning over the animals when, at Napoleon's call, nine great dogs enter and chase Snowball out of Animal Farm.

Napoleon, now with his canine bodyguard, assumes control and command, and changes some of their routines, though not without dissent. Squealer explains the motives behind these moves, and as no one wants to see the return of Jones, the animals go along with the new leadership. Boxer believes that Napoleon is always right, and vows to work even harder. The Sunday morning meeting is led by Napoleon and his lackeys, and the ritual Sunday parade is somewhat amended. Three weeks later Napoleon announces that the windmill is to be built after all. Once again Squealer cunningly explains away this change in policy and tactics.

Farmer and Stockbreeder Agricultural magazine, first published in 1843, and concerned with all aspects of farming, agriculture and livestock.
silage Preserved fodder.
basic slag A by-product of a steel-working process, rich in lime and used extensively as a manure.
incubators Here, an apparatus for hatching eggs by artificial heat.
cranks Mechanical term for arms on shafts for communicating motion to or from the shaft.
harrows The harrow is an agricultural implement consisting of a heavy frame set with iron teeth, and is dragged over ploughed land to break up and stir the soil, to root up weeds, or to cover in seeds.
Minimus The word is Latin for 'least'.

Revision questions on Chapters 3–5

1 Describe the attack on the farm by the humans, and the animals' resistance.

2 What is learned about Boxer in these chapters?

3 Why does Mollie desert the farm?

4 What were the opposing arguments of Snowball and Napoleon over building the windmill?

5 Why did Napoleon change his mind over the windmill (a) in your opinion, (b) according to Squealer?

Chapter 6

The hard work continues: Sunday work is imposed, and the building of the windmill involves serious exertions, especially by the indomitable Boxer. Shortages are evident, and Napoleon, not without protest, decides to undertake some trading with humans. A local solicitor, Mr Whymper, is to be the intermediary, and Squealer once again pacifies those animals disturbed by this new move. Animal Farm, though hated and suspected by most of the outside human world, does command some respect for its achievements so far.

The pigs move into the once forbidden farmhouse: as Squealer explains, they need the detachment and quiet to pursue their complex plans. The appropriate amendment is made to the Seven Commandments. In a November gale the half-built windmill is destroyed, and the renegade Snowball is exposed and cursed as the perpetrator. Napoleon, now styled 'The Leader', decides to start its rebuilding at once, in the name of loyalty to all that Animal Farm stands for.

Leader Stalin himself (see p.24) did not assume this title: but most of his contemporary dictator rulers did, e.g. Hitler (der Führer), Mussolini (il Duce) and Franco (el Caudillo).
broker Middleman to transact business and negotiate bargains.

Chapter 7

A bitter winter suspends building operations; but Boxer, in particular, is not dismayed. Food becomes short, but the outside world is deliberately deceived by various ruses. The hens are forced to surrender their eggs for sale, in order to buy grain and meal from outside. Napoleon, always surrounded now by his canine bodyguard, negotiates the sale of some timber to Pilkington and Frederick, playing one off against the other.

Snowball, apparently and allegedly, is behind every crisis and disturbance, and Squealer informs the animals that he (Snowball) is and always has been a traitor to the cause, much to Boxer's amazement. According to Napoleon secret documents have apparently been discovered establishing Snowball's guilt and complicity. The dictator later makes a rare appearance, and all those who had previously raised objections to his policies are attacked by his dogs. Boxer is assailed, but he defends himself successfully, whereas many others are killed. Some feebly confess to outrageous crimes against the system, and they too are torn to pieces by the dogs. For the workers, Animal Farm has lost some of its pride and wonder. The 'Beasts of England' anthem too is suddenly replaced by another, on the pretext that the Revolution has been achieved.

Black Minorca pullets A pullet is a young hen, especially from the time she begins to lay to the first moult; this breed of domestic poultry is so named as it is supposed to have originated in the Balearic island of Minorca.

coccidosis An animal disease caused by an internal parasite.

Revision questions on Chapters 6–7

1 How much time has passed so far since the beginning of the story? Indicate by quotation, or reference, how you have drawn your conclusions.

2 What is the major problem confronting the animals in the building of the windmill? How is this eventually overcome?

3 Why is Snowball accused of the windmill's destruction? What do you think caused its collapse?

4 Were the confessions of the accused pigs true? How do you know? Why did Boxer not kill the attacking dog outright?

Chapter 8

The Sixth Commandment has been suitably amended to cover the executions. The Leader, Napoleon, now rarely emerges, and when he does it is with full display and retinue. He occupies separate apartments in the farmhouse, and eats alone from the best crockery. His portrait adorns the wall of the big barn. Squealer regularly recites the statistical details of the farm's progress. Executions, and some confessions, continue; and still Snowball is seen behind every crisis, his memory being overlaid with tales of treachery and malice.

After much haggling, the timber is to be sold to Frederick: Napoleon, who personally conducted these lengthy negotiations and deliberate playing off of Frederick and Pilkington against one another, has trusted no one, and has thus gained enough cash to buy the windmill's machinery. In fact, Napoleon has been deceived: the notes are discovered to be forgeries, and Frederick indeed attacks the farm the next morning with fifteen men and six guns. No help is forthcoming from Pilkington, and the windmill is blown up by the human invaders. In a passion of revenge the animals attack the men and force them off: but many animals die in the fray.

To Napoleon and Squealer, however, this represents a victory, for they have driven off the enemy from their sacred soil. The dead are ceremonially buried, speeches are made, celebrations and new decorations are organized. The finding of a case of whisky by the pigs has interesting consequences, and leads to a further amendment to the Commandments.

Crown Derby A late 18th century porcelain made at Derby, marked with a crown.
title-deeds Documents containing or constituting evidence of ownership.
deadly nightshade A perennial and highly poisonous herb, otherwise called belladonna.

Revision questions on Chapter 8

1 Give an account of the negotiations leading up to the sale of the pile of timber: why were they so protracted and complicated?

2 Why did the human invaders destroy the windmill?

3 How and why does Squealer persuade the animals that they have won a victory?

4 What is the obvious implication of the Squealer and broken ladder episode? At what earlier part of the story was this, in fact, apparent?

5 Indicate the various ways in which Napoleon and his pigs have moved nearer towards human habits and failings.

Chapter 9

In the Battle of the Windmill Boxer had been the foremost fighter, and had, in fact, been injured, but he toils on despite his wounds. He is soon due for retirement. The winter is a cold one, and rations are reduced for all but the ruling pigs. Squealer finds arguments to persuade the rest of the animals that life is still better than it was under Jones's rule. The pigs develop and increase their already dominating influence, and clearly separated by rank and caste from the working animals. The education of the young is Napoleon's preserve and priority, and he organizes brewing for himself and his kind. New ceremonies and processions abound – organized 'Spontaneous Demonstrations' are held, with long recitals of statistics and details of Napoleon's prowess.

The farm is proclaimed a Republic, and the sole candidate for the Presidency, Napoleon, is duly elected. Boxer still works himself hard and looks forward to his pensioned retirement: but one day he collapses, and is taken off to the knacker's slaughter-house. Squealer elaborately details Boxer's treatment and death in hospital. However, Benjamin, Boxer's laconic old friend, knows better. The pigs hold a memorial banquet in Boxer's honour – and drink another case of whisky.

Chapter 10

Years pass: few now remember pre-Rebellion days. No one has been allowed to retire. The farm, however, has progressed materially, the pigs and the dogs sharing fully in its prosperity, although this cannot be said of the workers themselves. No criteria exist by which to estimate their present condition, yet the workers still take some pride in their unique status. The eventual universal Republic of Animals is still believed in.

One day, to the amazement and terror of the rest of the animals, the pigs emerge walking on their hind legs, carrying whips. The sheep have been taught a new slogan, and the Old Commandments have been abbreviated to one. The pigs have developed human tastes in many things now, including their reading and clothing.

A party of local farmers arrives one day, invited to inspect Animal Farm; that evening, the farmhouse is alive with noise and laughter. The working animals approach and peer through the window. Napoleon is at the head of the table, and the pigs and the humans are drinking playing cards and toasting each other's achievements and finer points. In a speech Napoleon announces various changes, including the renaming of the farm back to its original 'Manor Farm'. Speeches and gaming continue, and the watching animals are moving off, when a tremendous din bursts from the farmhouse. The watchers rush back to see Napoleon and Mr Pilkington at loggerheads, both apparently having cheated at cards, and everyone is shouting and angry. It has become impossible to distinguish the pigs from the humans, and the humans from the pigs.

rheumy Watery.
Muzzle Nose and mouth.
John Bull Established in 1906, this was a weekly magazine of family interest, including articles on current topics and personalities, short stories, serials and competitions. It changed its style and name (to *Today*) after the 1945 war, but failed to survive competition in the 1960s.
Tit-Bits London weekly paper, first of a long succession of periodicals designed to amuse and instruct; established in 1881.
Daily Mirror Morning illustrated newspaper, started in 1903 as a newspaper for women. It is designed to maintain a high popularity among the masses.
ratcatcher breeches Trousers, often gaitered and of unconventional cut, as worn by professional ratcatchers.
watered silk A silk with a wavy lustrous finish.
bon mot Witty remark.

Revision questions on Chapters 9–10

1 On what grounds, real and alleged, were the rations distributed unfairly?

2 What is the real function of the 'Spontaneous Demonstrations'? Describe them.

3 Why was Moses, the raven, allowed to stay?

4 Can you in any way account for Napoleon's treatment of the sick Boxer?

5 Why were the old hopes now considered 'contrary to the spirit of Animalism'?

6 In your own words give an account of what the working animals saw and heard through the windows of the farmhouse when the pigs were entertaining the local farmers.

The characters

Mr Jones

Fallen on evil days

It should be particularly noted that none of the humans in
Animal Farm emerges well: this is important, for Orwell nowhere
suggests that the 'Revolution' was not justified. It was a legiti-
mately angry attempt at release from bondage and servitude,
and all the humans engaged before, during and after the
Revolution are presented in a bad light.

Our first glimpse of Jones is as he stumbles drunkenly about
the yard, drinking a further glass of beer before going to bed:
the next, as he equally drunkenly fires off a random shot into
the darkness. Some excuse is offered for his disposition: but he
is a 'hard master', and he and his men are neglectful and lazy.
After his flight from his farm, Jones seems to spend most of his
time in the Red Lion. Any sympathy he might have expected is
not forthcoming as the neighbouring farmers, especially Pilkington and Frederick, seek to turn his distress to their own
advantage. Indeed everyone spreads wild rumours, even fantastic lies, about Manor Farm; partly through fear of the Revolution spreading and partly, no doubt, to justify and contrast their
own way of doing things. Notice that Foxwood (Pilkington's
farm) is neglected and overgrown, and that Pinchfield, though
smaller and better kept, is in the hands of Frederick, a tough,
shrewd, litigious and hard bargainer. Jones's armed return is
unceremoniously routed: he is flung into a pile of dung at the
Battle of the Cowshed. He does not re-enter the story after this –
except to be used by the astute pigs as the perennial threat to the
farm animals – and is known to have died in a home for
alcoholics in another part of the country.

Other humans are drawn equally unpleasantly and unflatter-
ingly, apart from Mrs Jones, who escapes from the Rebellion
and the story in one sentence. Mollie deserts to find service with
'a fat, red-faced man in check breeches and gaiters' (Chapter 5);
Whymper, the solicitor go-between, is 'a sly-looking little man'
(Chapter 6); Pilkington and Frederick are distrustful hagglers

and opportunists (Chapters 7 and 8), and they and their men destroy the cherished windmill, which for them symbolized an evil and a threat (Chapter 8). Boxer is taken away to the knacker's in a van driven by 'a sly-looking man in a low-crowned bowler hat' (Chapter 9); and the last scene of the animals and humans (Chapter 10) is, of course, the climax of the book, and at once the most revealing and satirical – if not savage – contrast of all.

Napoleon

Not much of a talker, but with a reputation for getting his own way

The whole of *Animal Farm*, apart from the first chapter, is a chronicle of the rise of Napoleon's power and tyranny, and thus the entire plot is a reflection of his character. His 'cult of personality', emphasized by his attendant parasites, reminds us of his namesake, the Emperor Napoleon himself, or another French autocrat, Louis XIV, whose maxim was 'L'Etat, c'est moi.' The entire book, then, must be read to plumb his character to its unlovely depths: but some points must be particularly closely observed and integrated.

Note first Napoleon's cruelty and callousness and indifference towards the rest of the animals, the 'lower classes', from first to last. Although the original inspiration of the rabble-rouser old Major, with his gospel of Animalism, was hatred and rejection of Man, it implied equal sacrifice and altruism on the part of all the animals involved: to this Napoleon never subscribes. He takes an early lead in his serving out the first post-Revolutionary rations (Chapter 2); sends for the paint to change the farm's name and write out the Commandments (Chapter 2); and begins his steady descent (or ascent, depending on one's point of view) by the milk episode (Chapter 2). Napoleon conditions the puppies until the moment is ripe, an obviously premeditated action (Chapters 2 and 5). Other examples of his acts of cruelty and indifference abound.

Secondly, it must be observed how he is corrupted by power, and eventually corrupted to that inevitable animal-human contact which is the fundamental denial of the original spirit of Animalism. Napoleon contracts many, if not most, of man's vices. During the three years in which he consolidates his personal authority, Napoleon assumes all seven of the Deadly Sins.

We witness his egoism and pride in himself and his regime; his wrath as demonstrated by his cruel acts, has already been noted. Napoleon's envy of Man's status and accoutrements can be seen in his inexorable and inevitable adoption of human ways. From the outset of his career, Napoleon's lust for power and dominion is obvious; on a more sensual level, one notes 'his favourite sow' (Chapter 10) and the consequences of being the only boar on a farm with four sows. His gluttony is apparent too, as is his avarice – far removed from the austerity of Animalism. As none of the pigs under his protection and example produces any food, nor does much in the way of manual work, the list is complete with sloth – the sloth of gradual self-indulgence, emphasized from the start by the pigs' improved sleeping and living conditions.

Napoleon is, of course, a perfect deceiver, cynic, agnostic and hypocrite. From the episode of the milk (Chapter 2) and the whole business of Snowball's windmill, to the 'education of the young' (especially dogs and pigs), the maltreatment of Boxer, and his final speech, Napoleon's treachery and dishonesty are apparent. 'Tactics' and expediency are all-important: the ends are self-aggrandisement, self-security, self-omnipotence, and all means must be subjected to these ends. Comradeship and fellow feeling – common decency – are all right for the masses, the lower classes. In his aloofness and splendid isolation, with supervisory tasks delegated to the rest of the pigs and protected by his dogs, Napoleon has crushed all resistance, mental and physical, to his regime. He has further permitted a hero-worship and cult of his own personality to develop in his own lifetime. Napoleon and his career exemplify the stock symbol of the dictator classical and modern.

Snowball

More vivacious . . . more inventive

Snowball, the young boar who has less depth of character than Napoleon but more vivacity and invention, is the practical disciple of Animalism, with a firm and ingenious eye on Animal Farm's self-sufficiency and austerity. Self-educated, he helps to frame (and indeed writes out) the Seven Commandments, and organizes the Animal Committees and literacy classes. Further, by dint of great thought, Snowball reduces the code of

Animalism to the comprehensive but brief dictum of 'Four legs good, two legs bad' – a brilliantly lucid compression. He is altruistic – even though he agrees, and here rarely with Napoleon, that the pigs alone should enjoy the windfall apples. By his mastery of Julius Caesar's tactics, and his own bravery in the forefront of the fighting at the Battle of the Cowshed in which he attacks Mr Jones and is wounded, Snowball leads the animals to victory and a firmer hold on their dearly-won farm.

Yet all his practical brilliance and personal bravery, and his firm grasp of the potential of Animal Farm, come to nothing when set against brute force. Napoleon believes in internal strength and not external revolutionary incitements: and Napoleon's own personally organized forces include the trump card of a militant bodyguard obedient to Napoleon alone. Snowball is expelled ignominiously and without ceremony, at the crucial moment when he might have won the day in a tactical and political sense. Henceforth he is the scapegoat: the traitor to the cause; the ally of the humans. Snowball is now cast as a renegade, a deviationist from the true cause.

Snowball is central to the plot, and suffers the fate of all revolutionaries who, however callous and unsentimental, are at least sincere in the pursuit of their aims and in their attitudes, but are opposed by hypocritical power seekers and exploiters. It is profitable, indeed necessary, to keep their image alive for some convenient time as a bogey, a threat, an awful example: eventually, even this historical falsification is dropped once its purpose is served, and they are as if they had never existed.

Squealer

A brilliant talker

Squealer is the modern propagandist and political courtier *par excellence*. He is the model Public Relations Officer (of the worst and most parasitical type, of course, in the least democratic systems of government), and his career is worth noting in detail. He is a porker: small, fat, healthy and shrill, a brilliant talker with a persuasive skipping movement and tail-whisk. He is one of the founder members of Animalism, helping Snowball write out the Commandments: and he is the apologist over the apple windfall harvest (end of Chapter 3). Here he claims that Science has proved the need for apples in a pig's diet, a diet which must be maintained if the pigs are to keep Mr Jones at bay. He is involved, one can be sure in the rear, in the Battle of the Cowshed: and later he is well primed with details to persuade the frightened working animals of Snowball's treachery and crime.

As Napoleon's immediate henchman, Squealer follows every shift and turn of events by incriminating Snowball and dwelling on Jones's possible return, and the scapegoat and the threat respectively have their calculated effect on most. Those who do not readily accept are marked down by his shifty and ugly looks and, through him, with his trotter on the pulse of events in every camp, are destined for execution. Squealer is an excellent reader and interpreter of statistics, but, when the next human invasion occurs, is 'unaccountably' absent during the actual fighting, though he later hails the bloody battle as a victory. Had it been a defeat, as one skilfully disengaged he would no doubt have remained unharmed in any retribution. He is, of course, involved in the whisky episode, which leads to the exposure of his activities concerning the altered Commandments (Chapter 8). His hypocrisy and pretence over Boxer's disgraceful treatment reveal and develop him further in a most unpleasant and distasteful light. But Squealer thrives, growing enormously fat in his high office, and his is the first terrifying example of the pigs' adoption of man's upright stance.

Ingratiating to his superiors, ever suspicious of the workers from whom his authority ultimately derives, he symbolizes the nastiest type of jack-in-office, the officious apologist-intermediary between the rulers and the ruled. One only wishes that far fewer humans would behave as he does in any society, bureaucratic or totalitarian; for he is, regrettably, a type we instantly recognize as having encountered sometime, somewhere, and always to our cost.

Old Major

A majestic looking pig

Old Major's moment of glory is contained entirely within Chapter 1, but 'his soul goes marching on', for he, however portentously and egotistically (as befits a revered, grave Middle White Boar), initiates the climate of opinion which leads directly to the Rebellion and all its aftermath. Old Major transmits the wisdom of his great age; he sees a Utopia once Man is banished, although his own lot and existence have been particularly happy with many privileges. He foresees uncannily more than he knows (such as Boxer's fate, in which the hand of man has no part), and he propounds those basic principles which eventually form the creed of Animalism in the Seven Commandments (only four of which, incidentally, are true commandments, the rest being statements of belief). Old Major also passes on the legendary sentiments of 'Beasts of England', with what must have been its curiously stirring tune and rhythm. He is soon to die: but his skill is exhumed (Chapter 5), and forms part of Napoleon's Sunday parade. Old Major is remembered as an inspiration by the ageing manual workers of Animal Farm. However, even the custom of parading past his skull is to be dropped – 'suppressed' is the word – and his skull re-buried with his memory by the highest authority, as even Napoleon claims not to know anything about him: an ironic perjury. Once the inspiration of Animalism, his memory is now dangerous, and what is known of him must be rewritten or quietly pushed into oblivion.

Boxer

The admiration of everybody

Boxer is the 'willing horse', literally and figuratively, whose limited intelligence – he is one of the masses – renders him credulous, easily duped and beguiled. Boxer is also a devoted fighter, even a martyr, to a cause he cannot fully comprehend; all he can understand is the freedom from servitude. Simple, tender, resolute in his simplicity, he is the hardest worker, the strongest supporter, the most stubborn fighter for what he has been told are his new rights. He surrenders his little straw hat as a token of his belief (Chapter 2); he works mightily at the harvest, and indeed at any task where his strength is needed, devoting himself utterly and blindly to the Utopian hereafter (Chapter 3); it is he who turns the tide of battle (Chapter 4), yet regrets his felling of the stablelad; and his vigour alone makes the building of the first windmill possible (Chapter 6). 'Napoleon is always right'; 'I will work harder' – these sum up in their simple and clear self-direction, his entire belief.

Boxer is disconcerted by the blackening of Snowball's character, and is thus marked down as a target by the corrupt power-hungry pigs, but here again his strength prevents his own death. Even at this terrible moment, acting out of an instinct for self-preservation, he does not kill his attacker outright, but awaits Napoleon's command and authority.

Boxer cannot be assailed while strong: the pigs have to wait until he is weak, and meanwhile his brawn is useful. The carnage (Chapter 7) is quite beyond his comprehension: the fault cannot lie in the leadership, but only in himself, and so Boxer determines to work even harder from that moment. He fights again for the farm's immunity from the hated two-legged humans; barely recovered from painful wounds (though looking forward even more to his impending retirement) he begins again his painful and excessive labours. The result is inevitable: he outbids his strength, and one of his lungs collapses. The masters whom he has faithfully served do not even visit him, but sell him off with callous indifference to the knacker's – the very fate old Major believed possible only through human agency. His last hours at his farm are pathetic indeed: only old Benjamin sees through the pigs' hypocrisy and heartlessness. They consider his death in the true spirit of the exploiter who has no further use for the weak and suffering, even though the weakness has been induced by faithful service in their cause, and without which they would not have assumed such power and authority. Boxer is at least spared the sight of the pigs' assumption of man's posture, and of the final irony in the single Commandment.

The portrayal of Boxer has been termed a 'sentimental comedy': this can only be true on the most cynical and least sensitive plane. Viewed as a symbol of the common people under a totalitarian system, duped and exploited, mentally conditioned in a servitude that poses as a greater freedom, too simple to think critically and thus easily overpowered by propaganda, Boxer is a figure of tragedy and of warning. He represents common decency – and its reward – in a totalitarian setting.

Clover

A stout motherly mare

At the start of the book Clover is a 'stout, motherly mare approaching middle life': we know from old Major's harangue that she has borne four foals, and from description that she is tender and protective. By the end of the story she is one of the few pre-Revolutionaries still alive: Clover is now fourteen years old and still works, despite her stiff joints and rheumy eyes. Like her counterpart and consort, Boxer, she is hardworking, patient, and an immediately faithful disciple of the gospel of Animalism. With Boxer she helped in that first crucial harvest gathering: of course, Clover could not equal Boxer's enormous physical efforts, but her mental endeavours exceeded his by some measure in that she did at least learn the entire alphabet, though not well enough to put words together. She partakes in the final assault party in the Battle of the Cowshed: she upbraids Mollie for her weaknesses and discovers her tokens of defection (Chapter 5). Clover is always kind and solicitous on behalf of others, and throughout warns Boxer not to over-tax himself. Her memory is just good enough to recall the original Commandments before their amendments, but her critical limitations prevent her from relying on her memory, and she remains a loyal and devoted, encouraging worker for Utopia, though troubled from time to time.

After the carnage of the purge (Chapter 7) in which, in her docility and non-resistance, she has been left unassailed, it is to Clover that the animals go for protection. This is a touching (and most important) scene, in which we share her very thoughts; and even her comfort in reminiscently singing 'Beasts of England' is cut short by new instructions from above. Clover remains steadfast to the end to the principles of Animalism, for she knows nothing else and knows of no other solution. The very final scene is witnessed through her dim eyes. If she could but realize it, her vision of the confused and interchanging faces of the men and pigs is the staggering climax and perplexity of simple humanity exploited by relentless and expedient propaganda, and thus one of the bitterest satirical exposures possible.

Benjamin

He saw nothing to laugh at

Benjamin the donkey is the arch-cynic: he is the only working animal who is not fooled by the Revolution and its leaders. The oldest animal, the most irascible and ill-tempered, Benjamin sees 'nothing to laugh at' in this world. He is a devoted, if silent, friend of Boxer, his apparent impassiveness and lack of demonstrative affection emphasizing that devotion. He continues as he has always done, working, but without doing anything extra. He can read, but 'there was nothing worth reading'. Benjamin fights gallantly enough and works hard in the building of the windmill, but he expects (and gets) no particular reward for what he has always done and has always been willing to do. That is his lot in life, and to expect anything else is to him foolish. He does not seek trouble: he is secretly amused at the humans' destruction of the windmill, for to him this is an inevitable consequence of the counter-Revolution (Chapter 8).

Benjamin alone, and at once, sees through Squealer's activities in amending the Commandments, though he says nothing. He will not interfere. However, when Boxer collapses and is taken off to the slaughterhouse (Chapter 9), Benjamin can contain himself no longer among the credulous fools who have allowed themselves to be beguiled into a condition where such situations and such hypocritical callousness are at all possible. At the end of the story he is still there: after all, as he says, no one has ever seen a dead donkey. But Benjamin is for ever soured and embittered after Boxer's betrayal and rejection in his hour of greatest need. It is fitting that he should read out the all-embracing single Commandment (Chapter 10): of all the working animals only Benjamin would appreciate its intolerable cynicism.

Moses

He told tales and did not work

Moses, the Jones's tame raven, is the sole absentee from old Major's speech: he is drawn darkly as a spy and a tale-bearer, lazy and yet a most persuasive talker about the afterlife of the animals in Sugarcandy Mountain. Moses escapes with his human protectors at the outset of the Rebellion.

He returns, unchanged, after several years, still endlessly talking about the haven of rest, peace and comfort, and he is thus some solace to the oppressed working animals. Now that the Revolution has been accomplished, at least as far as the dominant pigs are concerned, Moses is no longer a danger and an irritant: in fact, he can be tolerated as an object of the animals' curiosity. He affords them some compensation and consolation in their oppression and misery – however ironic and malicious in the circumstances. It is often the poor and oppressed, who have least on this earth, whose sole hopes lie in heavenly reward for their earthly misery.

Mollie

The foolish, pretty white mare

Mollie, the trap-mare, is one of the privileged classes on whom the initial austerity of the new regime falls very hard. Used to flattery and human affection, she does not fall into old Major's category of animals whose lives are miserable, laborious and short. Mollie hopes the Rebellion will not alter her vain and sophisticated way of life, or at least not overmuch. She is lazy, and remains fastidious; she learns only her own name, tastefully decorating its letters with flowers. She has no stomach for the Battle of the Cowshed, which she regards as an unwholesome and rather unnecessary brawl. Inevitably Mollie deserts Animal Farm, for she finds freedom in servitude to humans, who pander her with those conditions under which she prefers to live. She is no Revolutionary: there is no crusading ideal in her delicate soul. The Revolution has no use for such parasitic adornments, and after 'defection' or 'deviation' Mollie is never spoken of again.

General questions and questions on related topics for coursework/examinations or other books you may be studying

1 What are the most important elements in old Major's speech? What is so 'revolutionary' about his attitude and suggestions?

Suggested notes for essay answer:

A two-part question: deal with each separately.

1. Main elements:
    (a) Note first word 'Comrades' as a unifying, classless, all-embracing appeal from the dignified respected elder. The word is carefully repeated eleven times.
    (b) Major's role as wise old prophet sharing his long and bitter experiences (hence, as a legacy, the immediate subsequent dominance of the pigs).
    (c) He postpones the detail of his dream – good spell-binding 'button-holing' technique of the orator: the audience must wait, hence the increase of attention, interest, and tension.
    (d) Detail logically accumulated, mostly in short sentences, of man's gross inhumanity to servile animals: he stresses unnatural deprivation, greed and casual cruelty.
    (e) Reaches first climax: the solution to all their (hitherto meekly accepted) misery: a simple formula of release (later condensed to 'Four legs good, Two legs bad') the basis of their struggle.
    (f) Prophetic warning (he is not called Moses for nothing) about the acquisition of human vices.
    (g) The total equality of all animals stressed.
    (h) Then the second climax: the revelation of his dream – nostalgic recollection, culminating in 'Beasts of England' as a political anthem (like e.g. Blake's 'Jerusalem').
    (i) Has set the governing pattern of future policy and strategy.
    (j) The whole of the rest of the story consists of the application and then the gradual reversal of all these elements.

2. Revolutionary elements:
    (a) Again, the opening and repeated word 'Comrades' – the

stock appeal to the brotherly kinship of radical activists (such as the early Trade Unionists and especially of the founders of the Russian and other political revolutions).

(b) The stressed need for the total reversal of accepted conventional status. The exploitation of animal species by dominant humans not part of natural justice.

(c) Man as a 'race' must be overthrown, a vicious tyranny to be destroyed, by a long and dangerously bitter struggle, the emphasis on rebellion: all these are basic elements in revolutionary theory throughout the ages.

(d) The formulation of clear and concise basic principles necessary to achieve their revolutionary goal.

2 Summarize the entire story of *Animal Farm* within thirty lines.

3 What information can be gathered from the book about the life and habits of Mr Jones?

4 Why did Napoleon and Snowball not agree? How did Napoleon eventually gain the upper hand?

5 What overall difference do you think would have been made if Snowball had assumed sole power?

6 In what ways was Snowball so convenient as a scapegoat?

7 Trace the relationship throughout the story between Boxer and Benjamin.

8 For what reasons, do you think, is the whole story of Boxer so moving? Or do you not find this to be so and why?

9 What part is played in the plot by the humans Frederick and Whymper? How do they become involved at all with the 'rebel' animals?

10 Trace in detail the whole history of the eventual building of the first windmill.

11 Show how the attitudes of Clover and Mollie are contrasted: in your opinion, whose behaviour is the more correct, or the more understandable, and why?

12 Do you find Squealer a wholly unattractive character? Does he do well whatever he has to do? What helps him to appear so convincing?

13 What is the role in the story of Moses, Benjamin and the sheep?

14 Quote the Seven Commandments. Which of them are amended during the course of the story? Show what circumstances lead up to each alteration.

15 'All animals are equal, but some animals are more equal than others.' What do you think this means, illustrating your suggestions with ideas or incidents from the story?

16 What does the outside world think of Animal Farm? How does this opinion vary, and how does it affect the activities of the farm at different stages of its development?

17 What is meant by satire? Consider carefully how various virtues and vices of man are illustrated and satirized in the novel.

18 Where do you find the satire to be (*a*) the most, (*b*) the least biting? State clearly what is being attacked.

19 Apart from satire, what elements of humour have you found and enjoyed in the story?

20 Indicate by specific reference to incidents and characters where sympathy is directed towards the ideals and aspirations of Animal Farm.

21 Show how the book, at one level, succeeds in exposing the development of a totalitarian state.

22 What do you understand the critic to have meant when he wrote: 'If it (*Animal Farm*) is a satire, it is a satire not only upon revolution, but upon all human hopes, by one who has ceased to share them?'

23 'These animals came from a war-weary mind too near the end of its tether.' Do you agree?

24 'The appeal here is not to a playful mood, but to the intellect.' How far do you think this is true?

25 '*Animal Farm*, in spite of its charm and wit and its great power, seems to me sad, bitter, clever – and dead.' Comment closely on each part of, and then in general on, this criticism.

26 Describe a struggle for power or a rebellion in any book you have been reading.

27 Describe in some detail the most memorable incident in a play or novel you have read recently.

28 Write a story imagining that you are an animal who has been ill-treated by humans.

29 Compare and contrast the content of any two or three pieces of prose or poetry which deal with man's relationship with the animal world.

30 Show how an author uses the theme of corruption in one or more books.

31 You may have read some books or stories in which animals play a more significant part than the human characters. What do you think was the author's intention, in each example, in writing this way?

32 Write about a speaker in a story or play you have read who influences his or her audience in a particular way.

33 From your reading, show how at least two different authors have handled the themes of either close friendship or co-operation within a group.

34 From your reading describe as carefully as you can how the writer of a book or play has developed a theme or structure which leads eventually to a startling climax.

35 Indicate the parts played by any two or three minor characters in a play or novel you have been studying.

Further reading

George Orwell: A Literary Study, John Atkins (Calder & Boyars, 1971)

Orwell: A Collection of Critical Essays, ed. Raymond Williams (Prentice-Hall, 1975)

Orwell and the Left, Zwerdling (Yale University Press)

George Orwell, ed. George Bott (Heinemann Educational Books)

George Orwell, Jeffrey Meyers (Thames & Hudson Reader's Guide Series, 1975)

George Orwell: A Personal Memoir, T. R. Fyvel (Weidenfeld & Nicolson, 1982)

Orwell for Beginners, S. Smith & M. Mosher (Unwin, 1986)